High Performance Teams

High Performance Teams

A new approach

Russell Futcher

Copyright © 2020 Russell W Futcher
All rights reserved

Dedication

Warwick Foster

my greatest mentor

TABLE OF CONTENTS

Introduction
- How to use this book
- What's in it for you?
- What's in it for the staff?
- What's in it for the organization?
- What is a high-performance team?
- High-Performance teams are different
- What really low performance looks like?
- High-performance teams background

Chapter One. The high-performance manager
- Your profile
- High-performance management style
- Evaluate your management style

Chapter Two. Evaluating your team members
- The people you want
- The people you don't want
- Managing people out
- Recruitment
- Team member composition

Chapter Three. The process of change
- The Tuckman team cycle
- The Kubler-Ross change curve

Chapter Four. Health Checks

1. Staff Survey
2. Process and documentation
3. Intranet
4. Staff training

Chapter five. Team Building Workshops

Developing team characteristics

Workshop delivery

Management Practices

1. Management team meeting
2. 1:1 Mentoring session
3. The manager's toolkit

Teams and Goals

1. Introduction to high-performance teams
2. Where are we now?
3. Team common goal
4. Performance goals
5. Process and intranet
6. Roles/responsibilities matrix

Management Behaviours

1. Being professional
2. Team behaviours
3. Team rules
4. Developing your management style

High-Performance Team.

Management Techniques

1. How to build trust
2. How to earn respect
3. How to support and motivate people
4. How to have good body language and persuade people
5. How to develop charisma and your emotional intelligence
6. Managing conflict
7. The 80/20 principle
8. Having a go is mandatory
9. Smart email
10. Timeboxing
11. The half pager
12. Problem-solving
13. The art of creativity and innovation
14. Staff training sessions

Team bonding events

Evaluate the team's performance

Chapter Six. Summary

Fully empower your team members

Continuous support and motivation

Increase the workload

Key things to remember

Appendix A. Team Roles/Responsibilities Matrix

Appendix B. Staff Survey Questions

Introduction

"A small team of 'A' players can run circles around a giant team of B and C players". Steve Jobs.

There are a lot of books on building high-performance teams. Many are academic, others describe team characteristics and outcomes, but nearly all fail to tell you exactly how to go about building a team. This book is different, it spells out a step by step team building approach, that has been used many times. It provides a complete set of training handouts and explains how to use them in a workshop setting. It provides you with a realistic view of the timeframe required and how you can vary the timeframe to suit your own situation. Building a high-performance team is not an event, it does not happen overnight or in a week. It is a process and it that takes many months and requires a managed environment and workload upon which to practice.

This book teaches you how to become a high-performance manager with people leadership skills, which is vital as only high-performance managers can build high-performance teams. It then explains how to evaluate people for a position in your management team, and how to go about training those people to develop high-performance team characteristics. You then have the option of having your management team train their staff on the same behaviours and techniques that both you and they have learnt.

Much of the information about high-performance teams is simply wrong. Most of it is a pure myth or suggests that it is unattainable or is the purvey of only the largest corporations. The training industry doesn't help either, advertising high-performance team training courses that run for a week, nonsense. You can teach adults new skills in a week but not behaviours or the embedding of new management thinking.

High-performance teams can execute more quickly, make better decisions, solve more complex problems, substantially increase productivity and staff morale and do more to enhance creativity and the building of skillsets than any other type of team. They thrive on change, excel at everything they do and are true innovators.

Russell Futcher

The capability and productivity gap between ordinary teams and high-performance teams is enormous.

Every manager knows that their top two management issues are, 1) the need to do more with fewer resources and 2) a need to have a fast start-up/reaction time to new predominantly unplanned or previously unknown business needs. These two issues, along with funding constraints, dominate management thinking. This book can significantly improve your ability to manage these and other issues.

You may be considering this book because you are experiencing reduced revenues, loss of profits, poor customer service or just a poorly performing management team. Maybe you are not happy with your project delivery, or your customers are complaining about service, or your manager is dissatisfied with your teams' performance and your staff are demoralised, job satisfaction is low and staff turnover is high.

You can either keep managing the way you are or look for a new approach that helps alleviate these and often other hidden issues. Successful management regimes of the past created today's organizations that now defy traditional approaches to management. These companies have flatter organization charts; intricate matrixed reporting lines, many horizontal interdependencies; and employees who know their jobs, goals and competitors better than they did decades ago. In a market in which change is speeding up, the incentive for business to review its approach to management has never been greater. High-performance management and teams are proven solutions to today's management challenges.

"Recently, some private sector and government sector organizations placed a new focus on high-performance Teams, as new studies and understandings identified the key processes and team dynamics necessary to create all-around quantum performance improvements. With these new tools, organizations such as Kraft Foods, General Electric, Exelon, and the US government have focused new attention on high-performance teams." Wikipedia.

High-Performance Teams

Russell Futcher

How to use this book

This book can be used as a complete approach to rebuild your management team by working your way through all five chapters, or you can select individual chapters to get specific outcomes.

Chapter One.   Becoming a high-performance manager

To build a high-performance team you need to be a high-performance manager. This means learning how to change your current management style into a high-performance management style by adopting new management practices, behaviours and techniques. A high-performance management style is a combination of traditional management qualities and people leadership qualities. This style does can be taught and is not difficult to learn.

Chapter Two.   Evaluating your team members

Selecting the right people to be in your management team is fundamental to success. You will be investing a lot of time in training and developing these people. They in turn will be investing time in passing on skills to the remainder of the staff. This chapter leads you through a process of evaluating the suitability of the management team members, the ones you want, the ones don't and then provides recruitment tips for employing new team members.

Chapter Three.   The process of change

It is important to have a basic knowledge of the change process, the specific stages that we as humans move through and that need to be managed. The approach this book is based on takes the change process into account; it is a low risk approach that allows you to implement at your own pace.

Chapter Four.   Health checks

There are four assessments called health checks that are carried out to assess the workplace culture and activities that support a high-performance team. There are two people health checks, staff views of management and staff training needs, followed by two documentation health checks, process and documentation and intranet management.

The results give an invaluable insight into, 1) How management is viewed by staff; 2) The state of process and other documentation; 3) The use of an Intranet; and 4) Staff training needs.

Chapter Five.   Team building workshops

This chapter provides a detailed roadmap of comprehensive team building workshops with training handouts. Typically, it takes six to nine months to build a team. The outcome is not just a high-performance team but a healthy team where people are supported, motivated, recognized for their achievements, are committed to decisions and plans, and where there is genuine comradery between team members.

Chapter Six.   Summary

Management is all about our interrelationships with people. Within our professional sphere, most of us seek out someone who we see as a people leader, someone who takes an interest in us, that we are happy to follow, be loyal to and who makes us feel good about ourselves. High-performance management is all about people leadership skills, being that leader that others are seeking out. Finally it discusses empowering your people and key things to remember.

Russell Futcher

What's in it for you?

People who have worked in a high-performance management team describe it as a life experience never to be forgotten. You'll solve the top management issues, get the personal satisfaction of having acquired high-performance leadership skills. An all-embracing feeling of security and of being privileged, a genuine understanding of your value and how you may increase it, earned good feelings about yourself worth.

What's in it for the staff?

"A unique experience that connects people for the rest of your life". - Chris Judd, AFL Premiership Team.
Happiness stems from spending time with people we like and high-performance team members care and support their colleagues like no other team members. They can expect significant job satisfaction, more expansive career opportunities, comradery, being the best in their field and a good lifestyle. Working with people who are loyal, supportive and trustworthy, professional development, acquisition of new management techniques and behaviours. Over time becoming increasingly better at whatever is being done, the ability to overachieve in comparison to others.

What's in it for the organization?

Profits, ability to rapidly expand, market growth, having a management Team that focusses on business needs and growth, staff loyalty, being an employer of choice, reduced costs and vastly improved services delivery.

A staff member once told me, "I couldn't wait to get to work each day; we did fantastic things, couldn't believe I got paid to do it.

High-Performance Teams

What is a high-performance team?

Different characteristics have been used to describe high-performance teams. Some of these descriptions are listed below. For the purposes of this book, based on my experience, I define the key characteristics of high-performance teams as.

Management style.	A high-performance management style focuses heavily on professionalism, people development, and business performance.
Team meetings.	Management team and Team Members weekly meetings, that makes use a common standing agenda with meeting rules of behaviour.
Common goal.	Gives direction to all actions and acts as a measure of success after a task is complete.
Assist others with work.	After completion of their work, each team member should be willing to assist other team members with the completion of their work.
Defined roles/responsibilities.	When team members know what their roles and responsibilities are and how they support the team, and how they contribute to the success and results of the team, this produces greater job satisfaction and commitment.
Mutual accountability.	Team members must accept that they are accountable to each other, which guarantees better performance and excellence in teamwork.
Mutual trust.	High-performance team members have great trust in and mutual respect for their colleagues' ability. Everyone values and supports each other, and feedback is welcomed.
Open communication.	Keeping each other appraised on

	important matters, sharing fears and seeking counselling from each other. It is a higher form of communication based on trust and mutual respect.
Common behaviours and rules.	An agreed set of team behaviours and rules.
Shared leadership.	The whole team decides everything together, a behaviour of a mature high-performance team. Also different team members take turns in being the task owner and leader as the expert in the field.
Conflict management.	No team can progress until all team members absolutely believe that they have a voice that is heard. The team, as a whole, must settle and decide between competing ideas.
Decision Making process.	A good decision-making process can be used to diffuse conflict. Team members should agree on a method for the team to adopt
Time management.	Using techniques like the 80/20 principle, Mandatory, High-Desirable and Nice to Have, Smart email and Timeboxing.
Process.	Accept the need for all work to be process driven, locking down the operational environment and reducing the number of operational resources.

Table 1, High-Performance Team Key Characteristics.

Some other definitions.

"A high-performance team can be defined as a group of people with specific roles and complementary talents and skills, aligned with and committed to a common purpose, who consistently show high levels of collaboration and innovation, produce superior results, and extinguish radical or extreme opinions that could be

High-Performance Teams

damaging. The high-performance team is regarded as tight-knit, focused on their goal and have supportive processes that will enable any team member to surmount any barriers in achieving the team's goals.

Within the high-performance team, people are highly skilled and are able to interchange their roles. Also, leadership within the team is not vested in a single individual. Instead the leadership role is taken up by various team members, according to the need at that moment in time. High-performance teams have robust methods of resolving conflict efficiently, so that conflict does not become a roadblock to achieving the team's goals. There is a sense of clear focus and intense energy within a high-performance team. Collectively, the team has its own consciousness, indicating shared norms and values within the team. The team feels a strong sense of accountability for achieving their goals. Team members display high levels of mutual trust towards each other. "Wikipedia.

Scott Keller and Mary Meaney in 'Leading Organizations: Ten Timeless Truths' state that over a decade they asked more than 5000 executives to think about their "peak experience" as a team member and to write down the word or words that describe that environment. The results are remarkably consistent and reveal three key dimensions of great teamwork.

1. The first is alignment on direction, where there is a shared belief about what the company is striving toward and the role of the team in getting there.
2. The second is high-quality interaction, characterized by trust, open communication, and a willingness to embrace conflict.
3. The third is a strong sense of renewal, meaning an environment in which team members are energized because they feel they can take risks, innovate and learn from outside ideas.

Prachi Juneja of Dun & Bradstreet states that successful teams share several defining characteristics.

1. Everyone on the team talks and listens in roughly equal measure, keeping contributions short and sweet.
2. Members face one another, and their conversations and gestures are energetic.

3. Members connect directly with one another—not just with the team leader.
4. Members carry on back-channel or side conversations within the team.
5. Members periodically break, go exploring outside the team, and bring information back.

A good description of a high-performance team comes from an excellent work by Katzenbach, J. R. and Smith, D.K. (1993), The Wisdom of Teams. They state: "A high-performance team is a small group of people with complementary skills who are committed to a common purpose, performance goals and approach for which they are mutually accountable".

High-Performance teams are different

The use of teams has become commonplace driven by the need to be more competitive and driven by changes in business technology. Current team organizational structures facilitate complementary skillsets, project-based delivery, better decision making and innovative thinking.

1. High-performance teams are objectively more focused than other teams in the way they work together. They are also consistently aware of the broader organisational aspirations and needs with everything they do.
2. They measure their own performance, self-correct as needed and welcome any team members opinion of how an individual or the whole team can do better.
3. They are expert resource managers and have highly developed time management skills.
4. As an extension of other teams, they have a greater sense of commitment towards the common goal and individual performance goals which defines them as a team.
5. It's a partnership, where team members actively work to ensure everyone's success.
6. They possess 'a one for all and all for one' mentality. If one team member fails, the whole team fails.

High-Performance Teams

7. High performance teams are highly disciplined with a focus on mutual accountabilities, role and responsibility expectations which are clearly defined and defined common team rules and behaviours.
8. They use process to lock down tactical, operational and administrative activities leaving them free to concentrate on strategic, business growth activities and projects.
9. They fix problems once, not tolerating recurring problems.
10. They have superior people leadership skills.
11. They support and motivate all around them with equal measure.
12. Their job satisfaction level is off the charts as is their loyalty to their employer.

High-performance teams however overachieve compared to other teams. They have a specific set of characteristics that stand them apart, they develop a collective consciousness and have a 'one for all and all for one' mentality.

So how do they do this? To answer this question, here is a summary of how the approach in this book transitions an otherwise ordinary team into a high-performance team.

Approach summary.

1. Manager, high-performance leadership development.
    a. Teaches the Senior Manager how to build a personalised high-performance management style with people leadership skills.
    b. Next is training on new management practices, behaviours and techniques which focus on people management and high-performance team building.
    c. The Senior Manager (or trainer) then trains the management team.

2. Team members, high-performance leadership development.
    a. Teaches the team members how to build a personalised high-performance management style with people leadership skills.
    a. Next, new management practices, behaviours and techniques are introduced which focus on people management, time management and the need for process.

3. Staff, high-performance techniques training.
    a. Team members armed with their new behaviours and techniques then train their staff.

Transition.

The secret to a team jumping over the fence to get to the high-performance team side is the application of a high workload and the way in which work is carried out. As we all know, busy people do more and do it in less time.

How is this done? Firstly, we know from our own experience that when we have a lot to do and are pushed for time we focus on the essential elements of the task at hand. We accept that probably having completed 80% of the work (80/20 rule) that this is enough, and we can quickly move on to the next task.

The team members and their teams are now equipped with new behaviours and techniques that more tightly integrate the teams making the flow of work easier. Everything is in place to direct their attention and efforts away from operational work to strategic work. They are also now able handle substantially greater volumes of work more quickly, consistently and of a higher quality.

Without a consistently high workload, a high-performance team will simply not perform as designed or expected. The high workload, underpinned with new behaviours brings into play the use of the new management practices, and techniques, causing all involved to be more reliant on each other, more trusting, more committed and mutually accountable for all work. It enforces the adherence to process, facilitates true collaboration, it gets more people involved with a task when necessary, each of whom is committed to its success and it forges close work bonds and a prevailing attitude of 'all for one and one for all'.

Secondly, the performance of the team will substantially improve when multiple team members are focused on the same tasks. As work often involves many teams, this helps drive tighter, process driven, team's integration.

Outcomes.

High-Performance Teams

1. The business focus and orientation are now directed towards business needs and growth.
2. The management team is now employing high-performance management practices and techniques, staff morale has increased, roles and responsibilities for all staff are clearly defined and staff training is bought up to date.
3. Defined team rules and a set of acceptable behaviours are in place.
4. Communication at all levels has advanced, only honest, timely and high value information is being exchanged.
5. All work is now subject to process and how-to guidelines.
6. Meetings are now shorter, more focussed and people more happily attend.
7. All work is produced consistently and with higher quality.
8. The business is now able to handle a consistently increasing workload, doing more with less.

Russell Futcher

What really low performance looks like?

Even the lowest-performing workplaces can be moved to high-performance; to illustrate my point, I have included an example of low-performance workplace behaviours that were deliberately injected into workplaces by the CIA. What follows is an edited extract from a CIA guide ("CIA's Simple-Sabotage-field-manual Guide to subverting any organization with 'Purposeful Stupidity".) I have included this piece because aside from amusing, it does in fact describe some of the low-performance workplace behaviours I have encountered. Do any of these sound familiar to you?

"Organizations and Conferences. Insist on doing everything through "channels." Never permit short-cuts to be taken in order to expedite decisions. When possible, refer all matters to committees, for "further study and consideration." Attempt to make the committee as large as possible — never less than five. Bring up irrelevant issues as frequently as possible. Haggle over precise wordings of communications, minutes, resolutions. Refer back to matters decided upon at the last meeting and attempt to re-open the question of the advisability of that decision. Advocate "caution." Be "reasonable" and urge your fellow-conferees to be "reasonable" and avoid haste which might result in embarrassments or difficulties later on".

"Managers. See that important jobs are assigned to inefficient workers. Insist on perfect work in relatively unimportant products; send back for refinishing those which have the least flaw. To lower morale and with it, production, be pleasant to inefficient workers; give them undeserved promotions. Hold conferences when there is more critical work to be done. Multiply the procedures and clearances involved in issuing instructions, pay checks, and so on. See that three people have to approve everything where one would do".

'Employees. Work slowly. Contrive as many interruptions to your work as you can. Do your work poorly and blame it on bad tools, machinery, or equipment. Complain that these things are preventing you from doing your job right. Never pass on your skill and experience to a new or less skilful worker." CIA's Simple-Sabotage-field-manual Guide to subverting any organization with 'Purposeful Stupidity.

There are many organization's like this, that unfortunately are locked into the past with old, more administrative than management approaches. Rules and regulations and the minutiae of outdated compliance also force a particular way of working. They are workplaces that do not provide tea or coffee and who lock the stationery cupboard.

High-performance teams background

"High-performance teams gained popular acceptance in the US by the 1980s, with adoption by organizations such as General Electric, Boeing, Digital Equipment Corporation (now Hewlett Packard), and others. In each of these cases, a major change was created through the shifting of organizational culture, merging the business goals of the organization with the social needs of the individuals. Often in less than a year, HPTs achieved a quantum leap in business results in all key success dimensions, including customer, employee, shareholder and operational value-added dimensions." Wikipedia.

Chapter One. The high-performance manager

"The highest reward for a man's toil is not what he gets for it but what he becomes by it." John Ruskin.

Your profile

As a Senior Manager you should have a minimum of 10 years management experience, preferably across different business cultures. The more of the following characteristics that you possess the easier the transition to high-performance management will be, namely someone who.
1. Is always 'on', who exudes positivity and energy.
2. Is supportive and motivational.
3. Cares as much about their staff as they do about themselves.
4. Wants to develop excellent people management skills.
5. Is willing to develop some EI skills. (Emotional Intelligence).
6. Is driven but is not necessarily ambitious. (although ambition is fine.)
7. Wants to be successful.
8. Wants to be passionate about their work.
9. Is willing to learn about team dynamics and team building.

If you feel that this does not describe yourself, then you will find the management behaviours and techniques training even more helpful.

> The job satisfaction derived from achieving high-performance management is nothing short of substantial; it further alleviates many of the anxieties that business managers feel and will give you the confidence you need to manage constant and significant change.

High-performance management style

To build a high-performance team you need to be a high-performance manager. This means learning how to change your current management style into a high-performance management style by adopting new management practices, behaviours and techniques. A high-performance management style is a combination of traditional management qualities and people leadership qualities which are complementary and inexorably linked to each other This style does not come naturally, it is not an innate set of personal characteristics, but it can be taught and is not difficult to learn.

There is a saying "managers have staff, leaders have followers", however, high-performance managers have both staff and followers. For an organization to succeed today, it requires people that are good at both management and leadership and that's where high-performance managers come in. High-performance management is a combination of.

Traditional management qualities.
     a. Exist to plan, organize, control or coordinate.
     a. Executes specific areas within their responsibilities.
     b. Formulates and enforces policies to achieve business goals.
     c. Sets individual performance goals.
     d. Focuses on the short term.

People leadership qualities.
     a. Exist to serve, inspire and motivate.
     b. Strong focus on interpersonal relationships.
     c. Empowers team members and does not micromanage.
     d. Is a good communicator.
     e. Provides timely feedback.
     f. Supports and motivates.
     g. Helps create a common team goal.
     h. Mentors the team to lead them to their goals.

People leave managers, not companies. A manager who walks the talk cares about their team and develops their team builds loyalty. Getting into the trenches with your team and showing them you care matters. The high-performance management style focuses heavily on people development and inter-personal relationships.

People are appointed as managers for a variety of reasons, ranging from a promotion because other people respect them which indicates good people skills or being the last person standing for the job. Others pursue management positions to increase their remuneration. Managers more often than not do not receive any formal management training. If they have been lucky, they may have received a one-week course on Team Leader, Project Manager or similar training which is hardly sufficient.

Most managers learn how to manage based only on what they observed and were subject to by a previous manager, for better or worse; mostly worse in my experience. There are many people unfortunately who do not understand that they are simply not good managers, all they know is their previous managers style, taking comfort in at least having a model to follow.

> 'The goal of management training is to increase productivity of all employees by motivating and educating managers. As manager confidence increases, so can the ability of the manager to implement company strategies, mitigate internal conflict and train subordinates to perform better. According to Carter McNamara, MBA, PhD at Authenticity Consulting, management training can reduce employee turnover while increasing employee motivation." Jeffrey Glen. BusinessDictionary.com.

High-performance management style assumes.

1. There is no single, accepted definition of management or skillset that it comprises. That there is an operating assumption that anyone can do it.
2. Training directly effects a manager's morale and confidence, bringing about a feeling of being more secure.
3. Management training helps with the implementation of new organizational changes with the least amount of productivity loss. Managers in turn are better able to convey the need for change to team members.
4. A fundamental pillar of management is the employee relationship which is the most important single factor in employee engagement.

5. Engaged employees are motivated and supported by their managers making them more productive.
6. Disengaged employees are more likely to be unsupported, causing frustration and disruption.
7. Appropriately trained managers improve employee morale and retention.
8. Many companies only invest in management training for senior executives (i.e. leadership development), leaving middle managers to fend for themselves.

For example, I describe my management style as being "Open and honest, fair and reasonable, someone who employs the best people and who develops people to become professionals". It's this style I use every day to guide everything I do.

You have an opportunity now to think about your current management style, which is defined by how others see you. Most of us have adopted the management style of a former manager or a manager we admire. A good test of your current style is how relaxed you are dealing with staff about conflict and poor behaviours and how they in turn would describe you. How would you describe your own management style today? Try to write a description in one to two sentences and then rewrite it to how you would like to be perceived.

> People's names are important, when you have hundreds or thousands of staff, remembering names is difficult. You can forget a name up to 3 times and be forgiven, but you won't be forgiven for incorrectly spelling someone's name, that is tantamount to an insult.

Your management style is contagious.

The central finding of EI (Emotional Intelligence) research is that emotions are contagious, attitude and energy 'infect' a workplace for better or for worse. team members will emulate your management style and, other staff will be influenced by it. I was often described as having 'energy' that infected everyone around me, it was only because even in the face of adversity, my management style made me remain positive and confident and as a result so did my staff.

Team members and staff will copy the pace you set, the sense of urgency you create, work habits, arrival and departure times. They will copy your behaviours, ways of thinking, like using mind maps and whiteboards, the way you delegate, how you deliver on commitments and the trust you give.

Management style development techniques.

There are six essential management style techniques that you need to master to develop a high-performance management style. Managers that come from technical backgrounds where they have not always had the opportunity to build broad people management skills will particularly benefit from learning these techniques.

Practice one technique a week and then repeat until they become normal, daily behaviours. Practice makes perfect, it won't take long before they become habits. You should continue practising for up to three months before moving on to the team building workshops that teach the same eight techniques to the team members. The six management style techniques can be found in Chapter Five, Team Building Workshops, they are.

Behaviours.
Workshop 4.   Developing your management style.

Techniques.
Workshop 5.   How to build trust.
Workshop 6.   How to earn respect.
Workshop 7.   How to support and motivate people.
Workshop 8.   How to have good body language and persuade people.
Workshop 9.   How to develop charisma and your emotional intelligence. (EI).

You can of course look at any of the other workshops whenever you like. The remaining workshops are covered in Chapter Five, Team Building Workshops. Once you are comfortable that you have mastered these techniques, try to write in one to two sentences how you would describe your new management style.

> "Success is nothing more than a few simple disciplines, practiced every day." Jim Rohn's. 8 Best Success Lessons.

High-Performance Teams

Evaluate your management style

This is a good time to take stock of what you have achieved to date and to evaluate your progress. This evaluation assumes you have completed practicing each technique at least once and have put into practice the management practices.

Evaluation questions.	Result.
1. You have been working on developing your management style?	
2. You have started to build trust with the team members?	
3. You believe that you are earning the team members respect?	
4. You Have become far more motivational and supportive of team members?	
5. You have put into practice stress management techniques?	
6. Your body language now says that you are a confident, approachable manager?	
7. You feel that you are starting to develop your own brand of charisma?	
8. You are more attuned now to people's feelings?	
9. You have put together a manager's toolkit?	
10. You are regularly using a notepad to record work for team members?	
11. You are challenging team members about the causes of recurring problems?	
12. You have completed a roles/responsibilities matrix for your own position?	
13. The weekly management team meeting with standing agenda is now operational?	
14. You have completed the team member evaluations?	

High-Performance Teams.
Chapter Two. Evaluating your team members

"Everyone is needed, but no one is necessary". - Bruce Coslet, Coach, Bengals.

Selecting the right people to be in the management team is fundamental to success. You will be investing a lot of time in these people and taking them with you on the road to high-performance.

Know your people. As a manager in the organisation who wants to develop teamwork, you need to have a good understanding of your people. Spend time with them, talk to them. This way, you will come to understand what they care for individually, you will also discover what makes them tick.

The people you want

Rarely will you have the opportunity to create a new management team from scratch. The norm is that you inherit an existing team upon which to build. High-performance team members need to have particular attributes and exhibit specific behaviours; it's quite likely you will not get many if indeed any of these from your people upfront. Therefore, you need to develop the team to behave and think in concrete ways, some will excel, and some will not. Those team members who are not making the grade will need to be moved to a different position or be managed out. There is no room for them in the management team.

It has been my experience that around 20% of team members do not make the grade, but that leaves 80% who do. They respond positively to high-performance training that recognizes their value, provides feedback on performance, is supportive and from which they achieve significant job satisfaction. As the Senior Manager, it's up to you to lead by example, providing the right environment and developing the right culture.

The best high-performance people possess two key characteristics. 1) Gusto, meaning they show great energy, enthusiasm, and enjoyment that is experienced by them taking part in an activity and 2) Alacrity, meaning, they perform all tasks with speed and eagerness. These two characteristics are virtually mandatory.

High-Performance Teams

Gusto and alacrity come in different forms. One is the person who is racing around to get something done, and another is someone who sits quietly at their workspace but produces remarkable results in unbelievably quick time.

Desirable team member characteristics.

1. Possesses gusto and alacrity.
2. Has a happy outlook.
3. Has a "give it a go" approach.
4. Meets their commitments.
5. Is supportive and appraising of others.
6. Is curious and a good listener.
7. Respects meeting protocols. (Turns up on time, abides by meeting rules.)

You can test for gusto and alacrity, staff, of their own accord, quickly race to your office when called.

Don't expect that all of these characteristics will be evident from day one. Often, they aren't, especially if you have a highly demoralized or previously poorly managed team. What you are looking for is how the team members are responding to your new management style and the changes you are introducing. If you are doing the right things, 80% of people will start to respond favourably. It will take a little bit of time but correctly done it will happen.

Team members can be both extroverts and introverts. Extroverts are generally preferred because of their talkative, sociable, action-oriented, enthusiastic, friendly, and outgoing personalities. They are also faster decision-makers, more significant risk-takers and more innovative thinkers. However, I have found that having at least one or two introverts in my teams was a good thing. They tend to be more focused, observant, lower risk-takers that carry out a more detailed analysis of available information than their extrovert partners and they bring a conservatism and balance to decision making.

Complimentary skillsets.

The team needs to be comprised of team members with multiple and complementary skills. They need to possess certain industry knowledge, a set of appropriate skills matching that knowledge, and personals strengths that drive their individual work performance. These elements create synergies with other team members and is one of the things that makes high-performance teams highly-productive.

In the case of other teams, the scope of the job for each team member is narrowly defined and importance is given only to their individual specialised skills or competencies.

When building a business management team, you need a team member for each major business discipline (sales, marketing and so on) who also possesses the personal qualities shown next under 'Extraordinary team members.

Extraordinary team members.

Some employees are extraordinary; they have qualities that make a huge impact on their performance and the performance of others.

1. They Ignore their job descriptions. Well not completely, but they think and act outside their job description or fixed roles, they take little notice of it. When they encounter situations that require action, they act irrespective of their role or position. These are the people who get things done.
2. They are eccentric. Someone with a somewhat unusual personality, someone who is very comfortable in their own skin. They may seem odd at first, but pleasantly so. They tend to be very creative, good debaters and make for excellent team members.
3. Pull their sleeves up. When the going gets tough, these people have a trait of forgetting about who they are and rapidly becoming a member of the team when required. They recognise when things have become serious and change their behaviour accordingly.
4. They appraise others in public. When your manager says you have done a great job, it rings in your ears for the rest of the day, week even. These people effortlessly appraise their fellow team members in the same way, and they do it publicly.

5. They are self-motivated. These people come to work firstly for its enjoyment, to satisfy their passion and secondly for pay. They are often possessed of an overwhelming need to be successful and work to achieve it.
6. They recognise the need to be process-driven. High-performance is process-driven, some people get it, some don't. Process brings consistency, increased quality, cost-effectiveness and savings, reduced task and project timeframes. These people are the ones who off their own back work to make process better.

Qualifications and work experience.

University/college level qualifications are irrelevant in terms of high-performance outcomes. Some of the most brilliant, professional, high-performance people I have ever known had no tertiary qualifications whatsoever.

Ideally, team members should have around ten years' team leadership or management experience of reasonably sized teams, eight to ten staff are a good yardstick. Generally they will be early middle managers or good candidates for a middle management positions who can be developed for senior management positions like your own.

Management potential.

Do you see senior management traits in any of the team members? You are after all developing them to become high-performance managers. Some clues are people who think about others first, believe they are no better than anyone else, are personable, non-judgemental and hold themselves accountable. Often the best assessment is to observe their interactions with yourself and others and go with your gut.

Team roles.

Belbin's team roles are a way of understanding your team members. The roles are best used as a guide only to each team members preferred working style. It is worthwhile trying to match each team member to a Belbin role just to see how well balanced the management team is. The 9 team roles are summarized in the table below.

	Team role	Strengths	Allowable weaknesses
Action oriented roles	Shaper	• Challenging, dynamic, thrives on pressure • The drive and courage to overcome obstacles	• Prone to provocation • Offends people's feelings
	Implementer (company worker)	• Disciplined, reliable, conservative and efficient • Turns ideas into practical actions	• Somewhat inflexible • Slow to respond to new possibilities
	Completer finisher	• Painstaking, conscientious, anxious • Searches out errors and omissions • Delivers on time	• Inclined to worry unduly • Reluctant to delegate
People oriented roles	Co-ordinator (Chairman)	• Mature, confident, a good chairperson • Clarifies goals, promotes decision-making, delegates well	• Can often be seen as manipulative • Offloads personal work
	Teamworker	• Co-operative, mild, perceptive and diplomatic • Listens, builds, averts friction	• Indecisive in crunch situations
	Resource investigator	• Extrovert, enthusiastic, communicative • Explores opportunities • Develops contacts	• Over-optimistic • Loses interest once initial enthusiasm has passed
Cerebral roles	Plant	• Creative, imaginative, unorthodox • Solves difficult problems	• Ignores incidentals • Too pre-occupied to communicate effectively
	Monitor evaluator	• Sober, strategic and discerning • Sees all options • Judges accurately	• Lacks drive and ability to inspire others
	Specialist	• Single-minded, self-starting, dedicated • Provides knowledge and skills in rare supply	• Contributes only on a narrow front • Dwells on technicalities

Figure 1. Belbin team roles. University of Cambridge.

1. The shaper. Challenging, thrives on pressure, has the drive and courage to overcome obstacles. Enjoy directing attention to the setting of priorities and objectives to shape the way team effort is applied.
2. The implementer. Disciplined, reliable, conservative and efficient. Turns ideas into practical solutions and procedures.
3. The completer-finisher. Painstaking, conscientious, anxious. Searches out errors and omissions. Delivers on time.

High-Performance Teams

4. They make sure a sense of urgency is maintained, and that the job in hand is completed effectively and efficiently.
5. The co-ordinator. Mature, confident, a good chairperson. Clarifies goals, promotes decision making, delegates well. They will recognise the team's strengths and weaknesses, ensure that they play to everyone's strengths, and make the most of the team's resources.
6. The team worker. Co-operative, mild, perceptive and diplomatic. Listens, builds, averts friction. This person supports others by improving communication between members, highlighting and building on others' strengths, and underpinning any shortcomings.
7. The resource investigator. Extrovert, enthusiastic, communicative. Explores opportunities, develops contacts. This person relishes exploring, investigating and reporting on resources, ideas or developments outside the group, and is good at dealing with external forces and negotiation.
8. Plant. Creative, imaginative, unorthodox. Solves difficult problems.
9. The monitor-evaluator. Sober, strategic, and discerning. Sees all options, judges accurately. They are the analyser of problems and evaluator of ideas and suggestions.
10. Specialist. Single-minded, self-starting, dedicated. Provides knowledge and skills in rare supply. Someone who puts forward ideas of new methods or applications and who looks for possible breakthroughs to problems.

"An effective way to assess the relative strengths and weaknesses of a team and helps the team to understand ways in which it could improve performance. Developed by Meredith Belbin in 1981, following nine years of study and has become one of the most accessible and widely used tools to support team building. The team roles were designed to define and predict potential success of management teams, recognizing that the strongest teams have a diversity of characters and personality types. Has been criticized due to its potential oversimplification and 'pigeon-holing' of individuals. However, when used wisely to gain insight about the working of the team and identify the team strengths and weaknesses it can be extremely useful." University of Cambridge.

Russell Futcher

The people you don't want

These are the people who are not comfortable with the concept of being a professional. In my experience they are usually cowboys who ignore instructions and process and do as they please. Then there are terrorists, they actively look for situations they can make worse for the pure warped pleasure of it.

People who possess the characteristics listed below are not good team players. A word of caution, however, you need to ask yourself "Do they behave this way because of the current workplace culture?". If you suspect this might be the case, I suggest you assume they have the capacity to change and can therefore be considered as possibilities. Then there are other people who are just plain lazy and disinterested no matter what the culture. Don't waste time with these people, use the "Do you want to become a professional?" approach (discussed later) and performance manage them out as fast as you can.

Look for the following.
1. Do not possess gusto and alacrity.
2. Do not have a "give it a go" approach.
3. Fail to meet their commitments.
4. Do not support or appraise others.
5. Do not show any curiosity and are poor listeners.
6. Do not respect meeting protocols.
7. Do as they please.

> I walked into a new company one day to start a new assignment, as I was walking down a corridor having just arrived, a young man walked right up to me and asked if I was Russell Futcher, "yes" I replied. He then said, "don't think you're going to tell us what to (expletive) well do" and turned around and walked off.

Unprofessional.

High-performance and professionalism are synonymous. Some people are not interested in becoming a professional; they choose not to change their behaviour. There is no room for this attitude in the team. team members and staff for that matter need to decide upfront if they are interested in being developed into professionals. Personal biases and prejudices for example cannot be part of a professional persona, nor is there room for personal issues.

> "If you have people in your team who, despite coaching and conversations, still cannot see the positives in their role (no matter how much potential they show or how long they've been in your organization), remove them. It's time to move on. Similarly, employees should avoid negative colleagues." Andrew May – Performance Coach.

Job perks.

These people are more interested in the job's perks than they are in the job. Gen Y can be guilty of this. These people, believing they are highly valuable come to you demanding or strongly suggesting at least that it's in everyone's best interest to expand their remuneration package. They want to receive more flexible working hours, paid overtime, a personal use Uber account, to bring their dog to work, want company paid life insurance and the list goes on. What I like about these people is they declare their real agenda to you, which makes them easily identified as people you don't want. High-performance team members are in it for the job, the work, the experience, not just for the perks.

Russell Futcher

> I have encountered many managers who frankly should never have been given a management title. A particular applications development manager spent his entire time sitting in his office; he had never ventured out into the general staff areas. His only communication with the staff was issuing decrees via email and publicly, via email identifying individuals for blame for any problems. To see him you had to make an appointment which was usually refused. In another case, an IT Manager I came across would sit in his office on Monday mornings with his team members, and they would decide amongst themselves who they were going to bully that week. Another hated his staff so much that he always yelled at everyone and blamed everyone else for the department's failings.

Hostage takers.

A staff member that holds you hostage: These are staff who due to their many years of service are the only staff members left with specific systems or applications knowledge. They are valuable resources and they know it. Steps need to be taken in these situations to document what they know and to train up other staff. I have encountered many people of this type and, each has firmly believed that they are indispensable and therefore can do as they please. They ignore management directions, carryout unauthorised work, are often lazy and even go as far as to turn up for work when it suits them.

Give everyone a second chance. Discuss with them what your expectations are and that specific behaviours of theirs are unprofessional and have no room in your business. Then document the discussion in an email and copy them and Human Resources as part of a potential 'Performance Management plan' to manage them out. More often than not, they call your bluff, believing you won't do it.

In the majority of cases, I have happily terminated their performance based on their failure to meet my documented expectations and for failure to carry out there, again documented, job functions in a professional manner. Never has a business suffered any real issues as a result. After their departure move quickly to get an experienced contractor in to fill the gap until you can replace them with a permanent.

> I have also learnt to become suspicious of hostage-takers as several have been involved in dodgy and illegal dealings. At an Internet Service Provider, I managed out a hostage-taker who had hived off a healthy portion of customer accounts feeding the revenues directly into a private bank account. At a Technology company I found a Network Manager who was profiteering from selling off a portion of the company's bandwidth. At another company I managed out an Operations Manager for refusing to change his rude, demeaning behaviour, upon which he said that "the department will cease to function if I leave", and clearly it didn't. Hostage-takers cannot be tolerated, I take the view that if they were run over by a bus on their way to work and therefore became unavailable, life will go on.

Managing people out

When you do need to remove a staff member, this is made easier if the person concerned recognizes that they are not keeping up with or performing like their colleagues. They are usually having trouble adapting to the changing environment. More often than not, it is a relief for these people when they are removed as it removes their anxiety and stress.

Alternatively, you can use the "do you want to become a professional approach?" This is a most useful technique for managing out unprofessional and troublesome people by asking them if they want to become a professional and describing what that entails so they can make an informed decision. If they say "yes", give them a second chance, document the discussion and copy them and Human Resources. If it doesn't work out, you may need to provide them with one final opportunity else you have what you need to terminate their employment.

No matter how sound the reasoning, terminating a person's employment is an unpleasant experience. Always write a bullet point script in advance and stick to it. This makes the conversation easier to execute and keeps you on point and not distracted from the duty you have to perform. Remember it's not a negotiation.

Russell Futcher

Always have a human resource or another third-party present to witness the discussion.

Recruitment

I always looked for people whom I considered were better, more skilled or more knowledgeable than me in their discipline. Interviews are supposed to be a two-way affair, but unfortunately, the majority of job interviews become a one-sided interrogation, I ask the necessary job description questions and then have a casual conversation with the candidate.

Best practice I have found is to have the best team members do the recruitment, let the most talented find the talent. Also, instruct them to have an open conversation with the candidate. I always learnt more about someone by just chatting about the job, the company, the work, their expectations and aspirations. Some suggestions as to interview questions.

1. Ask the routine job description questions that you need to cover off.
2. Tell them you are recruiting for high-performance team membership.
3. Do they have a happy outlook, and do they look genuinely excited to be there?
4. Does their demeanour yell "I will give it a go"?
5. Ask them what the worst mistake is they have ever made.
6. Ask that if you don't employ them, what are you going to miss out on?
7. Ask them what the consequences of a failed commitment are?
8. Ask them to ask you a question you have never heard before.
9. Say something obscure and see if they question you about it.
10. Ask them what their plan is to become a professional?
11. What successes have they had, what failures?
12. Ask them what they think of the job description?

> When doing a reference check, there's only one question to ask: "would you employ this person again?"

Recruiting - a note on Gen Y's.

Generation Y - born 1982–2000. Gen Y work needs are compatible with high-performance needs. Look for particularly bright people who can see the career benefits of being a member of a high-performance team. Here are three different perspectives on Gen Y's.

"Teamwork is high on the agenda of generation Y. "Working as a team is high on the agenda and regular team meetings and collaboration with colleagues is preferred. Generation Y wants to be involved and included. They expect openness and transparency from management and colleagues and seek a team playing mentality within an organisation. They are tech savvy. A whopping 85 per cent of SME owners report they are happy with their Gen-Y employees' technology skills." Ryan Gibson. Understanding Y.

"Poor spelling and grammar and a failure to understand what constitutes appropriate corporate behaviour are the biggest bugbears, with almost 70 per cent of surveyed employers reporting dissatisfaction with their Gen-Y employees' performance in those areas. The communication skills of Gen-Y staff disappointed 48 per cent of SME owners. With all these shortfalls why would anyone hire a Gen-Y? For most employers, there is one obvious answer - they have no choice." "Once they're on staff it is important to constantly communicate with, train and "indulge" Gen-Y staff to build relationships and get them enthused about being at work. They're brilliant at grasping things. We have a lot of production spreadsheets and they can get on the computer and understand them after only a few hours training." Mike Preston. SmartCompany.

"Gen-Y can be brats. Don't let them be. Some of them have grown up with indulgent baby boomer parents and they're very demanding". I consciously try to identify and avoid the gen-Y brats at the interview stage by questioning candidates on their attitudes, family background, friends, their wardrobe and even their pets. If a brat does slip through the net, however, there is only one solution - get rid of them. I don't care about their skills or what they've studied – it doesn't matter if they've got straight As. It's all about getting a sense of who they are and if they're a good person." "Gen-Ys are a perfect fit for a business that is growing out of its skin and where job descriptions can change on a daily basis. They have huge amounts of drive and enthusiasm and get very excited about where the company is going, they want to know the vision and they'll go where you take them." Jo Nagle. Let's Launch.

> I was asked to sit in on a recruitment interview for an important senior management position. The interview was conducted by a HR representative, the company practice. The manager and I basically got little air time. One candidate was an experienced but very dispirited man and the other a young, enthusiastic and energetic fellow. It was clear to me who should get the job and I strongly recommended the younger man whom I thought would be perfect for the position. Unfortunately, the HR rep saw it differently stating that experience was essential. They appointed the older man who three weeks later was let go as the job was well beyond his capabilities. The younger man had by then been recruited elsewhere.

Team member composition

Having evaluated the team members for suitability, you can now finalise the team's composition, consider the following.

1. The number of managers is in the range of 8 to 12.
2. Each team member has a complimentary skillset.
3. Each team member has between five to 10 years' experience.
4. New team member positions.
5. IT support roles.
6. Merging teams or groups of similar functional staff.
7. Standardising titles and pay grades across the business and demonstrating career progression paths.

Actions.

1. Finalise the team composition.
2. Update the organization chart.
3. Update the team member roles/responsibilities matrix with changes to positions, titles and roles.
4. If you have determined at this stage that someone is unsuitable then without delay either redeploy them or performance manage them out.

Russell Futcher

I was asked to do a very difficult assignment by the Chairman of a large Insurance group for whom I had worked previously. I only took the assignment on out of respect for the man concerned, otherwise I wouldn't have touched it. His problem was that a certain very well-known consulting firm had completely taken over his IT department was proving difficult if not impossible to move them on (politics) and was costing him a fortune. My job was to do move them out and restructure the IT department to manage without them. I knew the IT department well, I had set it up many years before. This was going to be an extraordinarily difficult and politically sensitive job.

The day I arrived, whilst looking for the head of the consulting team I overheard a voice say something like "run faster this time" and with that I saw banana peel come flying out of a doorway into the corridor, followed by a distressed young lady who quickly grabbed it and ran back into the office. I stood in amazement, then the whole event happened again "do it faster", followed by the banana peel which this time I picked up. The voice, arrogant with a distinct accent made me guess it belonged to the very person I was looking for. I found her office, asked her if she was in charge, she replied "yes" and then told her she had 15 minutes to pack up her things and that she was no-longer required. After that I went about dismissing her team. Sometimes pennies do fall from heaven.

High-Performance Teams.

Chapter Three. The process of change

"Believe you can and you're halfway there." -Theodore Roosevelt.

The health check activities in Chapter Four, and team building workshops in Chapter Five, represent change. It is important therefore to have a basic knowledge of the change process. There are specific change stages that we as humans move through and that need to be managed. The approach this book is based on takes the change process into account; it is a low risk approach that allows you to implement at your own pace. I have used this approach many times and, in some cases, have completed the health checks and the team building workshops in as little as 6 months. This represents an aggressive timeframe but demonstrates that it can be done and is based on the concept that the busier people are, the more they get done and the shorter the timeframe.

Moving to high-performance is such a positive experience that I have rarely encountered any change process problems. Indeed the prevailing attitude is very positive as team members and staff alike can see the benefits and outcomes that will result. If you are making wholesale changes across all of all the business then understanding the change process is all the more important, I'm referring to changes such as.

1. Changing people's positions.
2. Moving people between teams.
3. Merging teams or functional groups.
4. Retiring legacy, business computer applications.
5. Outsourcing a team or department.

Russell Futcher

The Tuckman team cycle

The Tuckman team cycle is a view of change specific to new teams or new team members showing how new behaviours emerge. Bruce Tuckman first published his model of group dynamics in 1965 comprising the four stages: forming, storming, norming and performing. (e.g. 'See Figure 2').

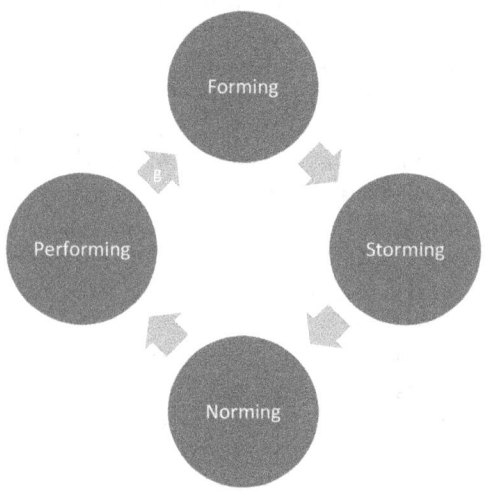

Figure 2, Tuckman's stages of team development.

Forming. The main difference between a random group of people and a team is the team's common goal. When individuals are first brought together, they do not have a common goal. They may be anxious about why they have been brought into this team; they will be hesitant about their new environment, unsure of what they have in common with other team members and confused as to the purpose of the project or program. Typically, the individuals will indulge in some superficial questioning of colleagues to look for more information, common ground and possible allegiances.

Storming. Different individuals will behave in very different ways during the storming stage with outbreaks of conflict being common between individuals or small sub-groups within the team. The more assertive individuals will try to impose some order by defining rules, resulting in leadership being challenged while a 'pecking order' is established. Assuming a common goal has been identified, very different views will arise as to how that goal should be achieved.

Norming. As the issues and conflicts of the storming stage are resolved, the team members start to settle down and concentrate on tasks and issues rather than personalities. An acceptance of shared values and behaviours develops with open communication that promotes constructive review and suggestions for alternatives. team members are starting to become a cohesive unit, genuinely working as a team with its capabilities being greater than the sum of its parts.

Performing. By this stage, the team is working as a focused unit. There is a collaboration between team members to solve problems with a visible change in mentality. There is a shared responsibility for the common goal and individuals are confident enough to innovate and provide insights into problems. team members demonstrate flexibility, with job titles become transparent and delegation of authority is working efficiently.

> "A High-performance team moves through the stages of forming, storming, norming and performing, as with other teams. However, the High-performance team uses the storming and norming phase effectively to define who they are and what their overall goal is, and how to interact together and resolve conflicts. Therefore, when the High-performance team reaches the performing phase, they have highly effective behaviours that allow them to overachieve in comparison to regular teams". Wikipedia.

The Kubler-Ross change curve

The Kubler-Ross Change Curve has been adopted into the world of organisational change from an unlikely source. Elisabeth Kubler-Ross was a Swiss psychiatrist who developed it in response to working with terminally ill patients. The Kubler Ross change curve works as a rough map to position employees on. Plus, it provides you with some simple steps for managing change and helping them move forward. One useful tool for leading change is the change curve. It provides a framework for mapping the emotions people are likely to be experiencing during different stages of the change management process. (e.g. 'See Figure 2.1').

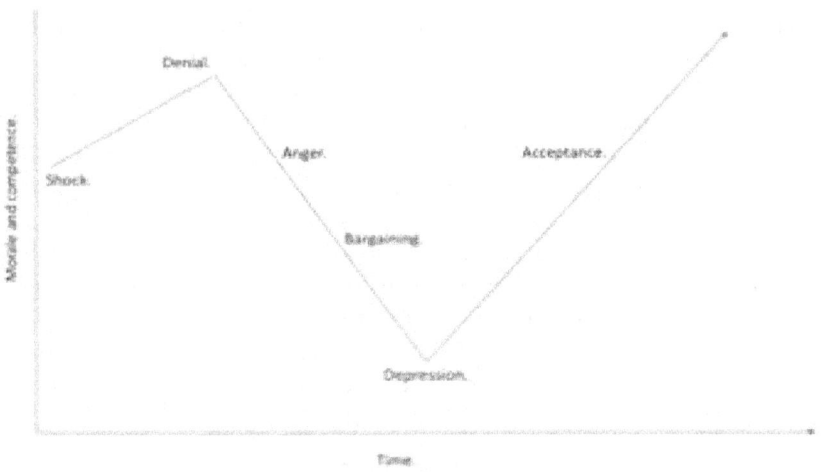

Figure 2.1, The Kubler-Ross change curve.

The stages of the Kubler-Ross curve. It is essential to understand that we do not always move along the stages step by step. People tend to move into stages in random order and may sometimes even return to a previous stage. Each stage can last for a different period, and someone can get stuck in a stage and not move on.

Shock. Surprise at the announcement of impending change.
Denial. This is the first stage and is mostly short-lived. team members may not be able to digest the fact that they are being asked to undergo a change. It can cause a reduction in productivity and a focus on the past. As Senior Manager, your role is to help employees understand why this is occurring and how it will be helpful. This stage requires communication with all questions answered.

Anger. When reality sets in team members and staff may begin to fear what lies ahead, turning into anger. This stage has to be managed very carefully as some employees may tend to vent their anger. Open and honest communication and support should be the focus. Given time this will pass away and make way for acceptance.

Bargaining. When team members and staff finally understand the change and realize how they must adapt, they may try to bargain with you, so that little is compromised. You cannot rush people into learning quickly or adapt to changes rapidly. You cannot expect 100% productivity during this stage.

Depression. This stage may not be a happy one for some team members or staff. This stage results in low morale and enthusiasm. It is important for you to appreciate that this stage is not easy for everyone affected. Training has an important role to play here, the more that is provided, the better to enable everyone to move forward.

Acceptance. At this stage, people begin to accept change, accept the situation and start moving forward. They accept and understand the need for the change. It's at this stage that benefits of the hard work put in by them so far start to materialize. The team is showing improvements now, and productivity begins to improve. It's now time to celebrate.

Dead car battery example.

One of the best examples of the Kubler-Ross Change Curve is the Dead Car Battery example. The following example demonstrates the transition process from one stage to another. It's a chilly winter morning, and it is dark outdoors. There is a thin layer of frost on the ground, but you are late for work and hence have to rush out to the car parked outside. As you place the key in the ignition and turn the car on, you realize that the battery is dead. What follows is a clear demonstration of a version of the Kubler-Ross stages.

1. Denial. Your first reaction is of absolute shock and denial. You cannot believe this happening to you when you are already running late, and you therefore try to start the car again and again.
2. Anger. Now that you realize the car cannot be started, you begin to feel angry and very mad at the situation.
3. Bargaining. Even knowing it won't help, you start asking the car to start, just for once. You promise it in your mind that you will keep it maintained and get the battery charged as soon as possible.

4. Depression. All the negative thoughts start rushing to your mind. You begin to feel depressed, sad and hopeless. You fear your job will be taken away and see no way out of the situation.
5. Acceptance. Now you figure out what you should do next. You can catch a cab and decide to deal with the situation later.

Considering the change curve can significantly boost the chances of successful business change because it addresses the key thing that makes change happen; people. If you can't bring people along with you, then your efforts for managing change will fail.

There are many Change Models, but the one that I have observed most often in practice is the Kubler-Ross curve. Each time you introduce something new, the team will move through or jump between these stages until a new skill or behaviour becomes the norm. As the rate of change increases, so will the speed of moving through the stages until the curve becomes normalised.

Chapter Four. Health Checks

You can't manage what you can't measure.

There are four assessments called health checks that are carried out to assess the workplace culture and activities that support a high-performance team, these are.

1. Staff survey. Views of management and the workplace.
2. Staff training needs.
3. Process and documentation management.
4. Intranet management.

Recording answers to questions.

Some questions may require a brief written response. However, in most cases, responses can be recorded in a spreadsheet, using a separate sheet for each health check heading.

Aim to keep the width of the spreadsheets to a minimum as this assists the analysis of the sheets by improving usability and readability. This process speeds up and becomes more intuitive as each of the sheets are worked through.

Format.

The health checks are comprised of 1) Actions, 2) Questions and next steps. These assess current work practices and identification of the work required to migrate from the current position to the high-performance standard.

Scope of works.

A scope of works needs to be created from the action results, and answers to the questions. The scope of works should then be broken down to a project task level and a project schedule be built using these tasks.

Russell Futcher

1. Staff Survey

A staff survey is an important health check that needs careful consideration. It measures 'staff satisfaction' and 'staff attitudes' toward management. Respondents should be allowed the option to be anonymous. Doing the survey is one of the healthiest activities you can do, but do not undertake one if you feel you cannot guarantee an appropriate follow-through. Asking the questions then failing to act on what staff have told you can be disastrous.

Survey steps.
1. Create the survey.
2. Conduct the survey.
3. Collate the results.
4. Determine what actions will be taken.
5. Chart and present the results.
6. Deliver on promises and monitor progress.
7. Provide monthly progress updates.

Appendix B shows a good example of a staff survey. Using a third-party survey provider like 'Survey Monkey' to create, conduct, collate and present the results is recommended.

Questions and next steps.
1. How do the staff rate IT management?
2. What needs to be done to address staff issues?
3. What do you think are the critical reasons for staff turnover?
4. Actions to be taken to reduce the staff turnover rate.
5. Actions to be taken to improve staff morale.
6. Email staff survey results.
7. Determine a management response and issue.
8. Top 3 staff issues to be worked on immediately.
9. Issue survey quarterly to update results and gauge management progress on resolving issues and requirements.

2. Process and documentation

The high-performance team standard for managing process, how-to guidelines and other documentation is.

Step 1. Baselined.

This step accepts that documentation templates may vary. A single, baselined version of each process, how-to guidelines and other documentation is required. Three rules are introduced to govern the use and control of all documentation.

1. Rule 1, If it is not baselined then it does not exist. All process, how-to guidelines and other documentation must be formally documented and baselined (finalised, ready for use).

2. Rule 2, The use of baselined process, how-to guidelines and other documentation is mandatory.

3. Rule 3, Only baselined documents are held on the intranet.

Step 2. CMM Level 2

This option includes Option A, plus the use of the Capability Maturity Model Level 2, (CMM Level 2). This is a process and documentation methodology applied to information technology and business project planning. The model describes a five-level evolutionary path of increasingly organized and systematically more mature processes.

1. Initial level: - processes are disorganized, even chaotic. Success is likely to depend on individual efforts, and is not considered to be repeatable, because processes would not be sufficiently defined and documented to allow them to be replicated.
2. Repeatable level: - basic project management techniques are established, and successes could be repeated, because the requisite processes would have been made established, defined, and documented.

3. Defined level: - an organization has developed its own standard software process through greater attention to documentation, standardization, and integration.
4. Managed level: - an organization monitors and controls its own processes through data collection and analysis.
5. Optimizing level: - processes are constantly being improved through monitoring feedback from current processes and introducing innovative processes to better serve the organization's particular needs." CCM Level 2.

One of the most significant benefits of using CMM level 2 is that a standard template is used for all process and other documentation. The template has a common look and feel, includes completion instructions for the user and complies with documentation management principles. Accordingly, all staff and especially new staff quickly learn how to use processes and other documentation in the most optimum fashion. It brings a consistency of approach, improves project quality, reduces cost by reducing the need for rework, improves estimates, scheduling and business outcomes.

Actions.
Record on a spreadsheet all the following document types.
1. Processes in use.
2. How-to guidelines or similar in use.
3. Methodologies in use.
4. Technical processes in use.
5. Project processes in use.
6. Work management processes in use
7. Reporting processes in use.
8. All other documentation in use.

Add spreadsheet columns to record document types that are.
1. Duplicated.
2. Redundant, old or dead.
3. Ad-hoc, not formalised.
4. Incomplete.
5. Drafts.
6. Not baselined. (finalised, ready for use.)

Questions and next steps.

1. Determine which documents will be kept and used for baselining.
2. What work is required to baseline the documents?
3. Determine which documents can be disposed of?
4. Which manual processes can be automated?
5. What work is required to create a standard, common documentation template.
6. Review all documents, rework as required and mark each as baselined when complete.
7. Identify umbrella processes that involve inter-team workflows, (activities where multiple teams are involved with the same task) and clearly define the end to end process, including hand-off points and deliverables.
8. Create a single version of each baselined document.
9. Convert baselined documents to the common template.
10. Load baselined documents onto the intranet.
11. Investigate moving to CMM Level 2.
12. Appoint a document manager as a role or position.
13. Train the document manager in document management principles.
14. Determine further works required and scope out.

3. Intranet

The high-performance team standard is that all process, how-to guidelines and other documentation are sourced only from the intranet as the 'the single source of truth'. The intranet is to be the repository of all business work practices and business memory. Smaller, team-based repositories are not allowed as they introduce the risk of duplication, lack of version control and non-adherence to process and documentation guidelines. It is not possible to have a high-performance team without a fully functioning and managed intranet.

For reasonably sized businesses (min 100 staff), a dedicated Intranet Administrator trained in document management is required. Documentation management principles and training for the administrator is essential. Having a library with examples within the intranet is required. Processes and other documentation under development need to be held under separate cover and not on the production intranet. The intranet needs to act as and meet the test of being the 'single source of truth'.

Actions.

Record on a spreadsheet all the following <u>intranet-based</u> document types.
1. Processes in use.
2. Guidelines or similar in use.
3. Methodologies in use.
4. Technical processes in use.
5. Project processes in use.
6. Work management processes.
7. Policies in use.
8. Other documentation in use.

Add spreadsheet column(s) to record document types that are.

1. Duplicated.
2. Redundant, old or dead.
3. Ad-hoc, not formalised.
4. Incomplete.
5. Drafts.
6. Not baselined. (finalised, ready for use.)

High-Performance Teams

7. Candidates for automation. (manual process that could be automated).

Questions and next steps.

1. Compare the 'Process and other Documentation' spreadsheet with the 'Intranet' spreadsheet. Determine which documents are to be kept for baselining and which are to be disposed of.
2. Identify umbrella processes that involve inter-team workflows, (activities where multiple teams are involved with the same task) and clearly define the end to end process that binds the teams.
3. What work is required to baseline the documents?
4. Which manual processes can be automated?
5. Build an business intranet.
6. Separate the intranet production and development environments.
7. Appoint as a role or position, an Intranet Administrator.
8. Create an intranet library of examples, (sample completed documents).
9. Close any team-based intranets or repositories in use?
10. Determine further works required and scope out.

4. Staff training

The high-performance standard is that all staff receive formal, supplier training for products they use. Staff training increases confidence in staff abilities and staff become qualified. The importance of training cannot be overstated. Companies invest substantial amounts on business infrastructure assets and services but often fail to train or fall behind in the training of their staff on the correct and most efficient use of those assets and services. Having untrained staff using business products and computer applications, is a risk.

By way of example, when a staff member who has been working on a product without training, then subsequently goes for training, this is what tends to happen.

1. The product how-to guidelines documentation gets updated.
2. New product functionality is used or used more correctly.
3. Business risks are reduced.
4. Security gets tighter.
5. Morale and confidence improve.

Questions and next steps.

1. Have all appropriate staff been trained on products and services
2. Are there individual staff training plans in place?
3. Is staff training up to date with IT applications and other technologies?
4. What is the annual staff turnover rate?
5. Is there a shortage of critical skills in the team?
6. Are skill shortages due to lack of staff, staff turnover and/or lack of training?
7. Can experienced staff mentor less experienced staff?
8. Create staff training plans and schedule training.
9. Update the team members and staff roles/responsibilities matrix showing required training courses.

Chapter five. Team Building Workshops

"Whether you think you can, or you think you can't, you're right." Henry Ford.

This chapter sets out a series of team building workshops and team bonding events as a roadmap of what to do to build your high-performance team. You have typically six to nine months to build the team. There is no rush, but remember, busy people achieve more, and the timeframe can be reduced. The outcome is not just a high-performance team but a healthy team where people are supported, motivated, recognized for their achievements, are committed to decisions and plans, and where there is genuine comradery between team members.

Scope.
Management Practices.
1. Management team meeting.
2. 1:1 mentoring sessions.
3. The managers toolkit.

Teams and Goals.
1. Introduction to high-performance teams.
2. Where are we now?
3. Team common goal.
4. Performance goals.
5. Process and intranet.
6. Roles/responsibilities matrix.

Management Behaviours.
1. Being professional.
2. Team behaviours.
3. Team rules.
4. Developing your management style.

Management Techniques.
1. How to build trust.
2. How to earn respect.

3. How to support and motivate people.
4. How to have good body language and persuade people.
5. How to develop charisma and your emotional intelligence.
6. Managing conflict.
7. The 80/20 principle and mandatory, highly desirable and nice to have.
8. Having a go is mandatory.
9. Smart email.
10. Timeboxing.
11. The half pager.
12. Problem solving.
13. The art of creativity and innovation.
14. Staff training sessions.

Developing team characteristics

The table below lists the common characteristics of a high-performance team and matches these against its developmental workshop. The workshops are designed to instil in team members new management practices, behaviours and techniques.

High-performance team characteristics.	Team building workshop.
Team meetings	Management team meeting.
Mentoring.	1:1 mentoring sessions.
Common goal.	Team common goal.
Performance goals.	Performance goals.
Effective working procedures.	Process and intranet.
Defined roles.	Roles/responsibilities matrix.
	Being professional.
Will assist other team members in completing their tasks.	Team behaviours.
Accept mutual accountability.	Team behaviours.
Practice mutually beneficial and honest communication	Team behaviours.

High-Performance Teams

Practice shared and interchangeable leadership.	Team behaviours.
A decision-making process will be used.	Team behaviours.
Shared values.	Team rules.
Complementary abilities.	Developing your management style.
Trust and mutual respect.	How to build trust.
Trust and mutual respect.	How to earn respect.
Motivational.	How to support and motivate people.
Open communication.	How to have good body language and persuade people.
	How to develop charisma and your emotional intelligence.
Conflict resolution.	Managing conflict.
High-performance technique.	The 80/20 principle.
High-performance technique.	Having a go is mandatory.
High-performance technique.	Smart email.
High-performance technique.	Timeboxing.
High-performance technique.	The half pager.
Problem solving.	Problem solving.
Creativity.	The art of creativity and innovation.
Shared leadership.	Shared and interchangeable leadership.

Russell Futcher

Workshop delivery

The workshops have been designed to be delivered by the senior business manager. They can however be delivered by engaging an in-house or external trainer. The best way to maximise the workshop results is to deliver the them via regular, one-hour sessions each fortnight.

Doing workshops fortnightly is best if you are going to cover all of them in six to nine months. This frequency gives each team member time to do some initial practice and to be able to provide feedback for discussion at subsequent workshops. You can as the situation demands, cherry pick the workshops to suit your own purposes.

The workshop sheets are designed to be used as handouts to facilitate the workshop delivery.

The workshops are designed to develop team members personal management styles, change their ways of thinking, instil new management practices and techniques, change their behaviours and improve their confidence as managers. As such, each workshop sheet states a specific outcome to be realised. These workshop outcomes represent the workshop learnings that in most cases need to become new habits.

It is important to consistently follow-up with team members (Management Team Meetings, 1:1 Mentoring sessions) that they are regularly practicing in order to form the new habits. In most cases the best time to put the outcomes into practice is at meetings and in conversations.

Once team members have become familiar and comfortable with the new behaviours and use of the techniques, they should then start running their own workshops to train their staff. A separate workshop discusses staff training.

The information contained on each workshop sheet is the minimum necessary to get the desired outcome.

Tailoring the workshop content or the desired outcome to suit local conditions is perfectly acceptable providing that you do not move to far away from the intent or outcome of the workshop. Note also that the workshops are designed to be delivered in the order that they are presented.

This process takes time and effort, try to relate each workshop subject to current events as it's crucial to be very clear on the learning outcomes you want from each workshop. Keep in mind that developing a High-performance team is not an event; it is a process.

Start slowly, continue to build up your confidence and familiarity with the high-performance concept and with a little practice, it gets considerably easier. Use the workshop sheets as handouts.

When running the workshops, consider the following.

1. The workshops are all about developing high-performance team characteristics and team member management styles.
2. What is it the workshop is aiming to do? (Introduce a new management practice, a new technique, a new behaviour?).
3. Given your own circumstances, what do you want the team to learn and what to do want them to do?
4. Try saying just enough on each topic to get the team to scrutinize the worksheet and then discuss it.
5. Always finish each workshop with acceptance of the outcome and how it will be implemented.
6. Encourage discussion about implementing the change.

> Success is nothing more than a few simple disciplines, practiced every day.

Russell Futcher

Management Practices

1. Management team meeting

There are three change forums available to help drive the high-performance team development, these are.

1. Management team meeting.
2. 1:1 Mentoring session.
3. Workshops.

If you don't already have a weekly IT Management Team Meeting, then you will need to establish one. This meeting, in conjunction with weekly 1:1 Mentoring Sessions and the Team Building Workshops, are crucial change management forums. Aside from meetings with your own manager, these need to be important events in your diary.

At the first (IT Management or team member) meetings, use the standard agenda.

1. Put in an item 'Moving to a high-performance' and handout the Workshop No 2 worksheet for discussion at the next meeting.
2. Challenge team members and staff to join you in moving to high-performance.
3. Advise that everything is up for review but that the future looks bright for all.
4. Discuss benefits for them and for the organization.
5. Hand out the 'Tips for a well-managed meeting' for discussion at the next meeting.

Make a point of noticing each Team/staff members reaction to the high-performance news, their reaction to the Workshop No 2 worksheet and 'Tips for a good meeting'. Try to identify early adopters (they look pleased at the news) and those who are surprised, maybe shocked.

High-Performance Teams

Tips for a well-managed meeting.

No one likes meetings, one of your challenges is to get team members to want to come along because this meeting has real value. Try these tips to change the way the meeting is run:

1. Ban the use of laptops; they are distracting. Insist on written notes and explain why. (see notepad.)
2. Try to meet in the same room each week.
3. Have presentation/video/communication facilities checked to ensure they are working before each meeting.
4. Have a rotating chairperson to allow each team member to gain experience with this skill.
5. Have a rotating minutes taker and or have the last person who arrives take the minutes. Arriving late is unprofessional. Minutes should only contain action items and should be issued the next morning after the meeting.
6. Absent team members to attend by video or phone.
7. No war stories, no discussions about similar experiences that don't add value.
8. Hold the meeting late in the day to allow for an open-ended finish time. As the team becomes more focused the meetings will get shorter, and a short meeting is a good meeting.
9. For long meetings, consider having everyone stand up for 15 minutes while continuing with the meeting. Standing up at meetings is also a very good technique for having a quick meeting.
10. Use a standing agenda.

A standing agenda contains the same subjects each week; it further acts as an agenda template that should be used by team members for their weekly staff team meetings. Adopting this approach is particularly important as it facilitates consistency of management approach and dissemination of information.

Russell Futcher

Management Team Meeting - (Standing Agenda)

Date.
Attendees.

1. Previous Minutes.
    a. Review actions from previous minutes.

2. Staffing.
    a. Poor performing staff, recruitment activities, current and planned training initiatives.

3. Service desk top 10 recurring problems.
    a. Around the table for comment about specific failures and new issues as shown on the reports.

4. Customer Satisfaction.
    a. An open discussion of any negative and or positive customer/user feedback received.

5. Major Projects.
    a. Update on performance (schedule, cost, delivery) of significant and business projects. Limit to projects that are running behind schedule.

6. Managed Services review.
    a. Issues, disputes, financial and outstanding matters.

7. Other Business. Around the table, open discussion.

8. Notepad. New work items from your notepad to be allocated to team members/staff.

9. Meeting Minutes.

High-Performance Teams

- a. Minutes are a formal record of the actions agreed to be taken during the meeting, discussion notes are not recorded.

- b. Minutes format is usually action/owners name/due date.

- c. A Decision Register can be created and attached as page 2 to the Agenda. Decision registers record team decisions which are otherwise lost in minutes. In all cases, each decision will have a home elsewhere, such as in team rules. The minute-taker is responsible for ensuring the decisions are passed on to the appropriate decision owner.

2. 1:1 Mentoring session

Hold a weekly 1:1 team member mentoring session. At each session include an informal performance review which could be as simple as just saying "I think you're doing a great job."

How to become a good communicator.

People leadership means being an excellent communicator, ensuring that the right message reaches the right person in the right way at the right time. Just doing the talking does not help, you need to concentrate on listening, which takes mental effort, communication is not a one-person show.

When speaking, consider.

1. Rehearsing in your head, the message you want to tell.
2. Putting yourself in the other persons shoes, how will they interpret the message?
3. Is the message clear, concise and unlikely to be misinterpreted?
4. If it is misinterpreted how will you back out?
5. Practice active listening, what is it the other person is trying to tell you?
6. Often if someone has a difficult thing to say to you, they will disguise it, not be clear or concise, you need to be on the lookout of this.
7. If the message (such as an employee's termination) is sensitive or unpleasant in nature, prepare a bulleted script for yourself to follow and stick to it.
8. Be frank, direct, open and honest, the other person will pick this up and be reassured by it.
9. Has the message been received?

During the session.

Try to diary at least an hour with each team member once a week. As each team member moves closer to high-performance, these sessions will become shorter or may cease altogether. Use this time as a mentoring session with your agenda in mind, namely that you are developing a team of professionals.

High-Performance Teams

Mentoring is a positive, supportive relationship, encouraging people to develop to their fullest potential. The scope of the sessions should change and evolve as the needs of the person being mentored changes. Using your situation as an example, aim to understand the other person's situation and out of work stresses and obligations. The day comes for all of us when personal events affects our performance at work. Everyone needs to be comfortable to be able to say something like "I'm just not operating at 100% at the moment, I have two sick kiddies at home and, it is taking a lot out of me".

The person being mentored should be encouraged to share information about his or her career path aspirations, be given guidance, motivation, emotional support and assistance with problems. If you have a new team or new team member; at the first session, try to exchange background information before you talk about anything else. Take the time to get to know each other, talk about moving to high-performance and the benefits.

Remember that without a mutually understood ability to speak freely, the relationship is unlikely to reach its full potential. Commit to honesty. Both parties should be prepared to offer frank feedback as appropriate, even if the feedback is critical. Listen and learn. Mentors, especially, need to remember that the relationship is not primarily about them. These sessions should reveal a team members preferred working style and as mentioned, professional aspirations. You are their role model, lead by example, remembering that your actions will create a lasting impression and will be copied.

Be careful of language; for example; I never criticize anyone even when the situation warrants it. Instead I tell people that I have an observation to make, albeit negative. The word 'criticism' or being perceived as being critical is negative; it turns people off; they stop listening and are unlikely to take on board what you have to say. If for example, you have made the same mistake yourself at some time or exhibited the same poor behaviour that you have 'observed' say so, its builds trust and reiterates that we all learn from our mistakes. Language is important. Always follow a negative observation with a positive one.

Russell Futcher

3. The manager's toolkit

As managers, we all have a personal folder that we carry around, usually with the current item we are working on or with papers we need for the day's meetings. Over the years through my many assignments, I have learned to carry some additional items as I found I was constantly referring to them to both raise and answer questions with staff who I would run into. Collectively I call these items my toolkit, I recommend you consider putting the same or something similar together as they prove very useful, when having conversations Referring to the items in the toolkit also shows staff that you have a genuine interest in them.

The toolkit items are very good ready reckoner's at meetings, the toolkit consists of.

1. A notepad.
2. An organizational chart.
3. A top 10 recurring problems report.

Notepad.

A valuable tool you are going to need is a pad and pen. If you walk into any business these days, you see a majority of people staring at their screens. Screens have a purpose for on-line collaboration, preparing presentations and documents and internet access. However, the ubiquitous laptop user takes more notes compared to those who use a pad and pen. Consider for a moment a study done by Princeton University and the University of California respectively, where students who took notes on paper learnt significantly more compared to their laptop peers.

Here's why; typing and writing use different cognitive processes. Research shows that laptop users type virtually everything they hear without processing the meaning of the notes they are taking. Typing is mindless transcription. Note-taking requires listening, paraphrasing, and listing of key points. Your cognitive process is more involved in the process of comprehension, and so this information is remembered better. Laptops are distracting, this may seem obvious, but still, the facts are staggering. Staff on average spend 40% of their time using all sorts of productivity killers, from instant chat messages to answering emails to merely browsing around the web.

I recommend you use a notepad to record notes, and comments you hear for follow-up. Issues you become aware of, information needs you have, new tasks, new projects, anything at all that you can delegate to a team member. The more you can record the better as you will need to delegate as much work as possible later on. The notepad will have an important role in keeping team workloads as high as possible. Record the item, who or where it came from, the initials of who you delegated it to and the date. Cross it out when completed and get back to the source of the item as required.

Organization chart.

The first thing I always ask for when I walk into a new business is an up to date organization chart. I think it's important that you have a copy with you at all times as there are so many discussions that come up with team members that relate to staffing. A useful chart shows a person's name and title, with a 'c' if they are a contractor, a total permanent count and a total contractor count. It keeps you familiar with the total number of staff you have, especially contractors who are expensive and tend to creep up in numbers. If you are experiencing a high staff turnover rate (anything over 8%), you can keep an eye on which areas are affected. Have a new chart created and distributed to team members monthly.

When talking with staff you can pull out the organisation chart and ask the staff member to point out where they are in the organization, what they are currently working on and what's their number one issue. It helps to show your interest in them.

Top 10 recurring problems report.

This is an IT service desk report, it has valuable information that you and the team members need to know. This report will keep you appraised of two things. 1. What is annoying the staff and customers. 2. How much resource and expense are you expending on recurring problems.

The 'Top 10 Recurring Problems' are things like applications reporting errors, data corruption, incorrect application field usage or the result of manual interventions by IT. Recurring problems create business disruption to the extent that the

Russell Futcher

business often puts in place manual workarounds, causing increased operational cost and decreased efficiency. The report should contain problem type, business team that logged it, IT team who owns it, date logged, the number of recurrences or times logged going back 12 months and the average time the problem has been open or unresolved.

When you get the report find out what's required to fix all 10 of the problems once only. This will flush out the real issues underlying these problems. IT is good at fixing recurring problems except that they keep coming back. The causes behind them can be anything from user training, broken process and application errors. Fixing the same problems time and time again or ignoring them, aside from being poor service, is just wasting resources. Finally, fixing these problems once and for all will improve staff morale. Keep an eye on them month to month.

High-Performance Teams

Teams and Goals

1. Introduction to high-performance teams

Predecessor action.
This worksheet requires customisation to suit local conditions before use.
E.g. '1. Why is it being pursued?'

Workshop.
A workshop to discuss why a high-performance team is being pursued, the steps to get there and the benefits.

High-performance is about being business focussed, understanding that the needs of the business always come before those of the team, or better, that both are synergistic.

1. Why it is being pursued.
    a. To raise the level of management competency and ability by the introduction of high-performance management practices and techniques.
    b. To address the management issues of the need to do more with fewer resources and a need to have a fast start-up/reaction time to new predominantly unplanned or previously unknown business needs.
    c. To address specific issues.
    d. To simplify the management of higher workloads.
    e. To prepare for a major strategic business initiative, such as an acquisition or merger or a new client.

2. What are the steps?
    a. Manager, high-performance management development.
    b. team members, high-performance management development.
    c. Staff training on high-performance techniques.

3. Business benefits.
    a. To be able to have more staff working on projects.
    b. Improve performance by making the whole of the business process driven, by removing redundant processes, tools, utilities, scripts and so on. By increasing automation, minimizing manual interventions, standardising wherever possible, tightly integrating the business teams and their workflows, bolster staff training, require a smaller business workforce and have more resources working on business strategic projects.

4. Personal benefits.
    a. More expansive careers, comradery, being the best in their field, good lifestyle, working with people who are loyal, supportive and trustworthy, professional development, new skills, knowledge and behaviours, and over time become increasingly better at whatever is being done, the ability to overachieve in comparison to others. High-performance training and attainment are something that very few people have the opportunity to pursue.

5. Organizational benefits.
    a. Profits, expansion, brand awareness and growth, having a team dedicated to the business, staff loyalty, employer of choice, innovation, cost savings, quality and vastly improved service delivery and reduced operational costs.

6. Job satisfaction.
    a. People who have worked in a high-performance management team describe it as a life experience never to be forgotten. It produces substantial personal satisfaction based on achievements and the acquisition of professional skills and knowledge. A feeling of being privileged where there is a genuine understanding of your value and how you may increase or change it. Happiness stems from spending time with people we like. The High-performance team membership effect is so profound that should a team come to an end, the reaction is one of genuine grief and a great sense of loss.

7. Timeframe.

High-Performance Teams

    a. High-performance team attainment is a process not an event. Typically it takes 12 months to achieve.

8. Background.
    a. "High-performance teams gained popular acceptance in the US by the 1980s, with adoption by organizations such as General Electric, Boeing, Digital Equipment Corporation (now Hewlett Packard), and others. In each of these cases, a major change was created through the shifting of organizational culture, merging the business goals of the organization with the social needs of the individuals. Often in less than a year, HPTs achieved a quantum leap in business results in all key success dimensions, including customer, employee, shareholder and operational value-added dimensions." Wikipedia.

    b. "Recently, some private sector and government sector organizations have placed new focus on HPTs, as new studies and understandings have identified the key processes and team dynamics necessary to create all-around quantum performance improvements. With these new tools, organizations such as Kraft Foods, General Electric, Exelon, and the US government have focused new attention on high-performance teams." Wikipedia.

2. Where are we now?

An introductory workshop to identify as closely as possible what type of team exists now, a 'where are we now?' exercise. Knowing the current position when compared to the target position gives insight into the gap and degree of change involved. If none of the five team types adequately describes the current team, the workshop should be used to define what the current team is by modifying one of the five types. This provides an opportunity for team members to share their views both good and bad about their current situation and what they want to retain and lose.

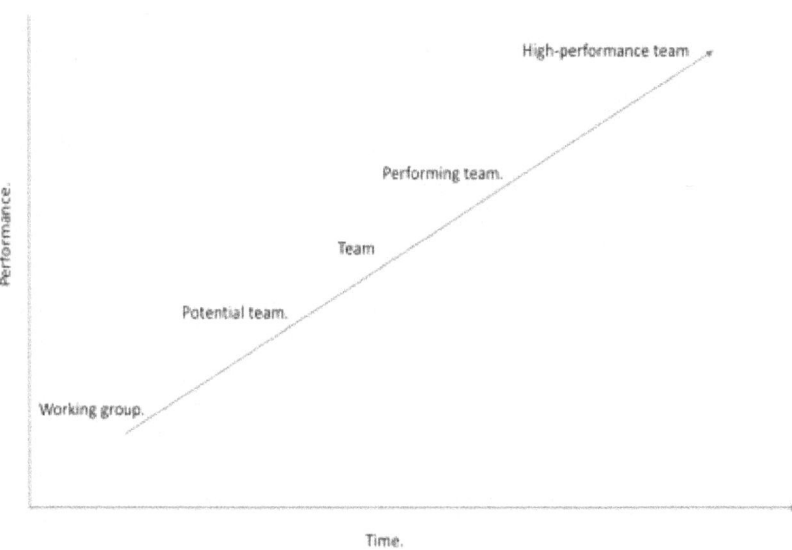

Figure 3. Team types.

1. Working group.

A group of individuals working beside each other displaying individual performance, action, purpose, and responsibility. They do not collaborate or take mutual action, they act selfishly, with each person only interested in what's in it for them. Characterised by.

1. A group of individuals with specific business skills.
2. No common goal.
3. No performance goals.
4. Absence of any real planning.
5. Unprofessional behaviours.
6. Reactionary with prevailing conflict.
7. Low productivity.
8. Siloed thinking
9. Influenced by politics.
10. Hold secret, private conversations.
11. Do not respect meeting protocols. (Turn up late, do not follow meeting rules).

2. Potential team.

These teams have started to work together but at a basic level. Enough collaboration regularly occurs that individuals work needs cross paths. Individuals still have their own interests at heart and care little for the interests of the group. Members may believe they are part of a team but are not yet acting like one. This may be because they don't want to take the risk of committing to a common goal and the mutual accountability that this entails.

1. A group bordering on a team with some coordinated effort.
2. Siloed thinking.
3. No common goal.
4. No performance goals.
5. Conflict is not managed.
6. Pecking order competition.
7. Hold secret, private conversations.
8. Influenced by office politics.
9. Do not take accountability for tasks.
10. Do not respect meeting protocols.

3. Team.

Issues and conflicts are being resolved and, work takes precedence over personalities. A common goal is evident but is more tactical than strategic. People start to settle down, activity integration and rudimentary or low-value information sharing emerges.

1. A team of business subject matter experts.
2. Common goal in place but competing views of how to achieve it cause it to fail.
3. Smaller silos that can be accessed by others.
4. Team members are starting to integrate their activities.
5. Taking ownership of and accepting responsibility for tasks.
6. Trying to respect meeting protocols.
7. Largely unprofessional.
8. Assertive, ego-driven individuals are trying to impose rules that benefit them the most.

4. Performing team.

The team starts to collaborate fully, skills and knowledge transfer is becoming common practice, shared leadership is being experimented with. Shared responsibility for others work is being experimented with as is the attainment of the common goal as people are starting to buy into it.

1. A team of subject matter experts with complimentary skillsets.
2. A common goal is in place but not everyone has bought into it.
3. Accepting accountability for work is starting to emerge.
4. Alacrity and gusto are evident in some team members.
5. Much greater activity integration and planning.
6. Actively stamp out office politics.
7. Assignment of blame has started to cease.
8. Problems are being managed as against just fixed.

9. High-value information sharing, and skills transfer is starting to occur.
10. Respect for meeting protocols.
11. Professionalism is emerging by default as against being planned.

5. High-performance team.

The high-performance leader stands out as the model to follow and copy, job titles have become transparent, a delegation of authority is in place, attainment of the common goal is driving all activity and is being actively measured. Behaviours are demonstrably changing. Team members are committed to one another's personal growth and development. Staff job satisfaction and morale is high.

1. Team Leader/Manager is the role model.
2. A common goal drives all activity.
3. Business needs and service delivery are priority one.
4. A team operating as a collective consciousness or single mind ('all for one and one for all').
5. Team members have shifted from a purely business orientation to a combined business expert and general management orientation.
6. Team member communication is at the highest level with personal fears being shared amongst team members.
7. Clearly defined roles and responsibilities are in place.
8. Team rules and the five essential high-performance team behaviours are in place.
9. Management practices and techniques are in place.
10. Team members exhibit gusto and alacrity; staff are starting to copy team members behaviours.
11. Mutual accountability is in place with team members holding each other accountable for team decisions.
12. Business practices have been locked down with effective baselined process and other documentation as the foundation of all work.
13. Cross-functional interfaces and alliances are much tighter.
14. A 'do it once only mentality and rule' is in place.
15. Team members are fully empowered and held accountable.

16. The team starts to measure their performance and self-correct as needed.
17. Meeting protocols are respected.
18. Substantial, high quality productivity is the norm.

3. Team common goal

Most teams are responding to a mandate from outside the team. But to be successful, the team needs to together develop its own common goal. The workshop outcome is the definition of a meaningful, measurable, common team goal.

Creating a common goal is important as it acts as a target goal to direct and motivate all staff. This gives direction to all actions and can also act as a measure of success after a task is complete. The common goal needs to take into account likely changes in the organization's business environment, competitors' movements and the future behaviours of consumers, combined with the team's own aspirations. Achieving the common goal should benefit everyone, especially financially as the business grows and profits increase.

A mistake that is often made is that teams define the achievement of becoming a high-performance team as a common goal, but that describes a result.

A common goal needs to be an outcome that comes from achieving a result. For example, achieving high -performance means that specific outcomes can then be realised. Examples of outcomes are improved service delivery, higher quality work, improved systems availability, increased organizational competitiveness, better consumer products, being an employer of choice or completing a major acquisition.

The best common goals merge organizational and team aspirations into one. The team common goal needs to be a goal the whole team will embrace and work towards in everything they do. An example of a good, measurable team common goal is.

High-Performance Teams

"Our objective is to transform the business into an agile and responsive customer-focused team, delivering quality solutions which meet the strategic needs of our business, in a timely and efficient manner." CML.

Or this one which was pertinent to the IT team concerned. "We are best when we fix the things you hate".

Everyone on the team knowing the common goal becomes committed to it and has a stake in it. When each team member and staff buy into the common goal and how their specific role contributes to it, productivity usually skyrockets.

Consider the following high-performance aspects.

1. High-performance teams have a clearly defined common goal which is then broken down into specific individual performance goals for each team member.

2. In high-performance teams, all team members are individually and jointly accountable for achievement of the common goal. Team members accept mutual accountability for the team outcomes whether success or failures. (one for all, all for one).

3. High-performance teams focus on the broader organizational mission and objectives. Other teams are entirely internally focused.

Things to consider.
1. What is it the business does?
2. How does the team serve the business?
3. What do team members functions have in common?
4. Does the common goal merge team and business aspirations?
5. How can achievement of the common goal be measured?
6. Is the common goal something that staff will be able to relate to?
7. Can it be applied to all activities?
8. Is it meaningful?

Practicing and measuring success.
1. How would following the team common goal be seen in practice?

Russell Futcher

2. How will you know if the common goal is being aimed for?
3. How will you know when the common goal has become effective?
4. How can you educate staff about the meaning and importance of the common goal?

4. Performance goals

Predecessor action.

A team members perfromance goals need to be established by the senior manager.

Workshop..

The workshop outcome is agreed individual team member performance goals that support and contribute to the achievement of the common goal.

Consider the following high-performance aspects.

1. High-performance team managers establish more challenging and ambitious performance goals for their team members as compared to the other teams. All the team members are supported and motivated to deliver excellence and are expected to be more passionate about the achievement of their goals.
2. Team members are empowered and motivated to take risks and pursue individual initiatives.

Performance goals need to.

1. Support the common goal.
2. Be clear. team members need to easily understand the goals they're working toward and why those goals are necessary.
3. Be measurable. The goal needs to have a measure within it to be able to know that it has been achieved.
4. Be realistic. The goals should be challenging, they should also be achievable.
5. Be on a timeline. When goals have beginning and end points, team members work to reach the finish line.

Examples.

1. Improve communication skills over next three months.
2. Implement management practices immediately and make behaviours and techniques habits within three months.
3. Increase team productivity over next 12 months.

4. Support and manage changes when they occur.
5. Improve staff retention rates over next 12 months.
6. Achieve sales of a certain amount in next six months.
7. Meet monthly budget targets.
8. Reduce advertising costs by end of first quarter.

Exercise.

1. Each team member to review their performance goals with the team to look for overlaps and synergies.

5. Process and intranet

Process.

The workshop outcome should be an agreement that all work, whenever feasible be process driven, meaning that.

1. Each process ranges from the beginning stage till the end for completing tasks.
2. All process and other documents should have a common look and feel.
3. All processes and documents are housed on the team or business intranet or knowledgebase.
4. All process, how-to guidelines and other documentation must be formally documented. (Rule: If it's not documented then it does not exist.)
5. When process, how-to guidelines and other documentation are baselined (finalised, ready for use) their use is mandatory. (Rule: The use of baselined documents is mandatory.)

The benefits of business process are consistency of results, reduced cost due to the lack of rework, increased productivity, lower expenses, improved compliance, agility, measurability, employee satisfaction and mitigated risk.

Process is important because it describes how things are done and then provides the focus for making them better and how they are done determines how successful the outcomes will be.

High-performance team aspects.

1. The members of a high-performance team work together to discover new work approaches and practices for attaining the best possible performance standards and benchmarks.
2. They understand that ineffective processes and procedures prevent the team from being efficient and can cause team members and staff to spend time fixing tactical or operational matters when their time should be focussed on strategic matters.

3. They know that ineffective processes cause problems with collecting, arranging, and evaluating information, while at the same time they hinder creativity, innovation, and risk-taking.

Intranet.

The workshop outcome is an agreement to have a single team or business intranet, to act as the single source of truth. All process, how-to guidelines, and other documentation are sourced only from a business intranet or knowledgebase. The intranet is to be the repository of all business work practices and business memory. Smaller, team-based repositories are not allowed as they introduce the risk of duplication, lack of version control and non-adherence to process and documentation guidelines. It is not possible to have a high-performance team without a fully functioning and managed intranet.

For reasonably sized businesses (min 100 staff), a dedicated Intranet Administrator trained in document management is required. Documentation management principles and training for the administrator is essential. Having a library with examples within the intranet is required. Processes and other documentation under development need to be held under separate cover and not on the production intranet. The intranet needs to satisfy the test of being the single source of truth.

Questions.

1. Is there a business intranet or corporate knowledgebase in use?
2. Is there an Intranet Administrator in place either as a role or position?
3. Are process and documentation development outside of the intranet?
4. Is there old and redundant content?
5. Is there a library function?
6. Are there any team-based intranets or repositories in use?

6. Roles/responsibilities matrix

This workshop clearly defines team member roles and responsibilities.

Predecessor action.

Prior to this workshop, issue to the team members blank roles/responsibilities templates along with the example in Appendix A. Have the team members complete their copies for their position and bring them along to the workshop. The workshop outcome is an agreed roles/responsibilities matrix for each team member ensuring there are no unnecessary overlaps or conflicts. Additional rows can be added to the matrix as required.

When team members know what their roles and responsibilities are and how they support the team, and how they contribute to the success and results of the team, this produces greater job satisfaction, commitment, and productivity. Have each team member talk in turn to their completed sheet. This activity is one of the most crucial activities to be undertaken, allow at least 2 hours.

Roles/Responsibilities Matrix.

Name.	Position holders name.
Position/Title:	The primary job function such as infrastructure manager, service desk manager.
Goals:	Individual performance goals or KPIs.
Accountabilities:	Position sole accountabilities, such as staff retention, sales targets, advertising campaigns.
Responsibilities:	Position shared responsibilities, Human Resources, Warehouse management, Purchasing.
Second, in charge:	Name of the staff member who is

Russell Futcher

	second in charge.
Roles:	Roles, titles such as Office Manager, Security, Fire Warden.
Ownership:	List the names of processes for which this person is the responsible owner and decision-maker.
Expertise:	Names of business functions/disciplines that this person has key knowledge of.
Training completed:	Course names completed.
Training required:	Course types.

Aim to get a team's table onto a single A4 landscape sheet as this aid's useability and readability.

Review, modify and agree the entries on each sheet. Check that individual performance goals are consistent with the common goal. You can also use the sheets to identify where you are lacking back-up staff who may also require training. The completed team members roles/responsibilities matrix should then be made available to all staff. At staff team meetings, team members should hand out blank roles/responsibilities' matrix templates to all staff for completion, review and agreement.

Management Behaviours

1. Being professional

A workshop to discuss what being a professional means. The outcome of the workshop is an agreed, shared definition of 'professionalism' for the team, a personal target that each team member agrees to pursue.

High-performance and professionalism are synonymous and becoming professional is within reach of everyone who commits to pursuing it. Any workplace or team can be moved to high-performance, as it's all about developing a team of professionals with the right skills and behaviours. Team members need to decide up-front if they want to become a professional in their chosen field.

What does it mean to be professional? Development of specialised knowledge, theoretical foundations, intellectual development, use of techniques, knowledge, competence, honesty, integrity, respect and accountability as well as self-regulation are some of the aspects that characterize professionalism.

It means that personal biases and prejudices, for example, cannot be part of a professional persona, it does not allow personal issues to play a role in a team as they can cause a team to fail. Even though team members should be concerned and caring about each other, this does not extend to displays of personal emotions or blackmail.

Things to consider when defining team professionalism.

1. Having a professional attitude. Being upwardly supportive. Not participating in secret or negative conversations. Arriving at work on time and staying until the day's work is complete. Putting in extra time when required.

2. Demonstrating professional maturity. Producing quality work. Acknowledging mistakes without shifting blame. Owning up to issues and presenting solutions. Being predictive about problems, acting before they occur to avoid them.

3. Managing time and work space. Maintaining a diary for appointments and deadlines, checking regularly to stay on schedule with meetings and tasks. Using smart email management techniques. Organizing your work space so that its clean and that files are organised.

4. Practicing leadership skills. Making presentations, chairing the CAB, being a business liaison contact, joining a professional society. Being up to date with industry changes by attending seminars and reading professional publications.

5. Communicating in a professional manner. Being aware of body language, eye contact and your handshake. Speaking clearly and matching the tone and speed of your voice to match the other persons. Practicing active listening.

6. The definition of professionalism you decide upon can be used to manage staff who are exhibiting unprofessional or troublesome behaviours.

Practicing and measuring success.

1. How can you put into practice the shared definition of professionalism?
2. What behaviours do you need to adopt or change to be considered a professional?
3. What other things can you do to claim you are a professional?
4. What feedback will help you recognise that your behaviours are those of a professional?
5. How will you know when your behaviours have become habits?
6. How can you educate staff about becoming a professional?

2. Team behaviours

Potentially a two-hour workshop to discuss the adoption and implementation of the five essential High-performance team behaviours. The workshop outcome is agreement to implement the five essential high-performance behaviours.

These are mandatory behaviours that need to be adopted and practised until they become normalised as habits. The application of increased workloads embeds and enforces these behaviours, so as the team moves closer to achieving high-performance these behaviours are expected to become more evident.

1. **Will assist other team members in completing their tasks.** In case of other teams, the responsibility of task and resource allocation, planning and coordination lies primarily with the manager and the team members act as per the instructions and guidelines of the manager. Each team member has an obligation to fulfil their responsibilities, be accountable for their actions and to complete their allocated work. After completion of their work, each team member should be willing to assist other team members with the completion of their work. Selfless collaboration is perhaps the finest quality of a high-performance team - people working together to achieve any task, each other's goals and the common goal. In high-performance teams there is a very high level of initiative, sharing of ideas and cohesiveness amongst the team members. The members of a high performing team act as business partners and they enjoy a higher degree of flexibility to achieve work goals. The entire planning and coordination are done by the team members collectively instead of being undertaken by a manager exclusively.

2. **Accept mutual accountability.** Team members must accept that they are accountable to each other, which guarantees better performance and excellence in teamwork. The team members have achieved high-performance when each team member is confident and comfortable about themselves in the team setting to praise the skills, work and achievements of the others.

3. **Practice mutually beneficial and honest communication.** This doesn't just refer to discussions during a meeting or other work activities, but also keeping each other appraised on important matters, sharing fears and

seeking counselling from each other. It is a higher form of communication based on trust and mutual respect. Team members engage in a frequent communication for discovering newer or improved ways of reaching their own goals and the common goal, resolving differences by collaborative problem-solving and sharing of experiences. In high-performing teams, dialogue and active listening are expected to be the norm. It is important to remember that misunderstandings can be a good thing, because they prevent groupthink.

4. **Practice shared and interchangeable leadership.** There are two aspects. The first is where the whole team decides everything together, a behaviour of a mature high-performance team. The manager must decide how soon and how much latitude will be given to team decision making. For a period of time, the buck needs to stop with the manager as the final arbitrator, but the target of shared leadership is the aim. The second is depending on the task the team is currently working on, different team members take turns in being the task owner and leader as the expert in the field, others follow their orders and instructions, no questions asked.

5. **A decision-making process will be used.** A good decision-making process can be used to diffuse conflict. Team members should agree on a method for the team to adopt, with practice something like the following should become normalised and intuitive.

    a) Clearly and unambiguously state the objective or goal.
    b) Collect available information and evidence.
    c) Consider the consequences of the proposed decision.
    d) Make a final decision.
    e) Is the decision low risk or high risk, if high risk, what risk mitigation needs to be put in place?
    f) How does it reflect on team members accountabilities?
    g) Is it consistent with the team culture?

3. Team rules

A workshop to define a set of team rules. This is a case of less is more, with no more than 10 rules at most.

The establishment of clear ground rules will give the team its cultural baseline and is a fundamental step in high-performance development.

In the case of a new team, rules also help to remove the inevitable confusion and anxiety that usually exists as new team members get to know each other. The rules come into play from the day they are agreed.

Examples.

1. We share a common goal.
2. You need the Senior Managers permission to die. (for the humour value).
3. Neglecting your family is unacceptable.
4. We actively support our staff.
5. Everyone has a voice.
6. If it's not written down, it doesn't exist.
7. Problems are fixed once.
8. Be prepared to present evidence.
9. Always conduct yourself professionally.
10. Ensure that our work standards comply with industry standards.
11. Asking for and offering help is expected.
12. Failure is ok; having a go is what's important.
13. If you can say it all in the email subject line, all the better.
14. management submissions are restricted to half a page.
15. Our team is non-hierarchical, and we are non-competitive.
16. It's not what you say, but how you say it.
17. Sometimes it's ok to ask for forgiveness than for permission.

*Attach a copy of the team rules to the Weekly Management Team Meeting agenda.

Russell Futcher

Practicing and measuring success.

1. Where and when will the rules be applicable?
2. How will you know if the rules are working?
3. How will you know when following the rules has become normal practice?
4. How can you educate staff on the rules?

4. Developing your management style

A workshop to get team members to think about their individual management styles, how they want to act and how they want to be perceived by others. The workshop outcome should be a one to two-line statement that describes each team members target management style.

People leave managers, not companies. Consider a manager that walks the talk, cares about their team and develops their team, builds loyalty, gets into the trenches with their team and shows them that they care. The team members need to understand that their staff will copy their style, what they do and say is important. Management style Is contagious; they must lead by example.

A high-performance management style focuses heavily on professionalism, people development, and business performance.

Example: "Open and honest, fair and reasonable someone who employs the best people and who develops people to become professionals".

You have an opportunity now to think about your current management style, which is defined by how you want others to see you. Most of us have adopted the management style of a former manager, for better or worse. A good test of your current style is how relaxed you are dealing with staff about conflict and poor behaviours and how they would describe you. Instinctively we know what people think about us and what type of manager we are.

Following workshops discuss some essential management techniques that need to be mastered in order to develop and achieve a high-performance management style.

Team members most of the time come from a business management background where they have not always had the opportunity to build broad people management skills. Rather their management acumen is judged on their business expertise and knowledge.

Russell Futcher

Your management style is contagious.

The central finding of EI (Emotional Intelligence) research is that emotions are contagious, attitude and energy 'infect a workplace for better or for worse. team members will emulate your management style and, other staff will be influenced by it. I was often described as having 'energy' that infected everyone around me, it was only because even in the face of adversity, I remained eternally confident, and so my staff did as well.

Team members and staff will copy the pace set by you, the sense of urgency you create, work habits and arrival and departure times. They will copy your behaviours, ways of thinking, like using mind maps and whiteboards, the way you delegate, how you deliver on commitments and the trust you give.

Practicing and measuring success.

1. Can you summarise your management style statement down to a few key words to help you remember how to act?
2. How will you know if your management style is having the desired effect?
3. How can you encourage your staff, in their case, to think about 'work' styles?

Management Techniques

1. How to build trust

A workshop to discuss how to build trust. The approach is to strike a balance between appearing as warm and competent so that you come across as credible and also human. Staff are generally aware of their managers business background, namely, the credentials that gained them their current management position

With credibility established, it's now time to demonstrate some vulnerability and show that you are indeed a fallible human being. The combination of competence and warmth will make you seem more trustworthy. If you want people to trust you demonstrate your knowledge and capability, then show them your human.

Counsellors often employ one of three tactics when first meeting a new client, they spill their coffee, drop their pad or embarrass themselves somehow to show they are fallible. By making yourself vulnerable, it is possible to build trust quickly. You must demonstrate your credibility first before you exhibit vulnerability; otherwise, it doesn't work.

High-Performance Team aspects.

1. High-performance team members have great trust in and mutual respect for their colleagues' ability. Everyone values and supports each other, and feedback is welcomed.
2. The members of a high-performance teams share a very high sense of camaraderie that develops over time.

Things to consider.

1. Virtual or distributed teams that need to establish trust, improving communications and managing conflict in the absence of face-to-face time.
2. To earn trust, you have to demonstrate trust.
3. Trust means making yourself vulnerable
4. Trust must be accompanied by accountability.

5. Trust someone until such time you have evidence that you can't.
6. Set expectations for a team culture based on trust
7. Trusting your intuition.
8. What are the most potent outcomes of a trusted environment?

How to rebuild lost Trust.

Sometimes we accidentally say or do the wrong thing and can lose the trust we have built up. Here is a quick solution.
1. Act quickly.
2. Be candid.
3. Accept responsibility.
4. Apologise.
5. Outline a remedy.
6. Don't blame.

Practicing and measuring success.

1. How will you know that others trust you?
2. Should you give trust first before receiving it?
3. What feedback will help you assess your trustworthiness?
4. How can you develop trust in others?
5. Is there a relationship between trust and making a commitment?
6. How will you know when others cannot be trusted and what will you do about it?

2. How to earn respect

A workshop to discuss how to earn respect. You need to show respect first; experienced managers know that respect isn't an entitlement linked to a job title.

Things to consider.

1. Lead by example. Demonstrate the qualities and characteristics you expect from the people you manage. It's essential to exhibit the traits you want others to adopt, such as honesty, creativity, being forthright, industriousness.

2. Be humble. No-one cares about where you went to school or past successes. Egotists are boring and turn people off. Get over yourself and do it quickly. Avoid conversations that entail self-promotion; they are obvious and do damage to your reputation.

3. Show commitment every single day. Get into the trenches with the troops and get your hands dirty with team members as often as you can. Work alongside them. Work longer and harder than they do. Get out of your office and visit staff workplaces. Talk to the staff, get to know their names so you can address them personally, ask them how things are going, ask what their top 3 issues are, make a note for follow-up.

4. Share your expectations of others. People want to know what your expectations are of them, that way they can work to meet or exceed expectations.

5. Help people succeed and advance. Help team members gain exposure and give them opportunities for development and advancement. Be a mentor, focus on those people who are bright, hardworking, dedicated, reliable and creative, and have skill sets that you don't, or those who show potential. Mentor them at work or support programs that allow them to earn a new skill or certification.

6. Balance delegation: keeping tight control of everything deflates employees and tells them that you don't value or trust their judgment, try to find the middle ground.

7. Teach and encourage creativity. It's expected that team members should take calculated risks. Recognise and discuss failure noting that having a go was more important than not.

8. Recognise success. Institute a team member and broader staff recognition program, such as a monthly 'best performance' award for someone who exceeded all expectations. People want to receive credit for a good job, especially in front of their others.

9. Compromise. Compromising is not weakness; nothing could be further from the truth. Managers who can compromise come across as caring and someone who puts others before themselves and who appreciates understanding a differing point of view.

Practicing and measuring success.

1. Do you need to act to gain someone's or your staffs respect?
2. How do you know that people respect you?
3. Where can the techniques be practiced?
4. How will you know if the techniques are working?
5. How will you know when the techniques have become habits?
6. How will you educate staff on this technique?

3. How to support and motivate people

A workshop to discuss the number one people management skill that you need to become well versed in, namely supporting and motivating your staff. The workshop outcome is acceptance of the six points on motivating staff.

Managers who actively support and motivate feel closer to those whom they are helping. By showing a sincere interest in your staff, you are building trust and inspiring others to achieve higher levels of performance.

Things to consider.

1. Every time you speak with a team member is an opportunity to provide feedback on their performance and to offer support and motivation. Everyone needs to receive positive feedback so that they understand that they are important, are a contributor, a team player and believe they are receiving an honest assessment of their performance.

2. Implement programs to recognise the performance and efforts of all staff. (Employee of the month).

3. When you give staff a difficult task or one outside of their skillset, remove the fear of failure by telling them that what you expect is that they 'have a go', not what they achieve, and offer to help.

4. Accept mistakes.

5. Do not make criticisms but instead make an unfavourable observation.

6. Give effective recognition for a job well done by doing it in front of others. Be sparing; however, recognition must be deserved.

How to quickly de-motivate people.

1. Lack of recognition, support and motivation.
2. Lack of autonomy or overly micromanaging.
3. Making decisions about team members without consulting them.

4. Allowing team members to miss commitments without a negative consequence.
5. Not making allowance for personal factors and their effects on work.

Practicing and measuring success.

1. Where and when can you practice this technique?
2. How will you know if the technique is working?
3. How will you know when the technique has become a habit?
4. How can you encourage staff to adopt this technique?

> One of the most important management functions is to support and motivate team members. A negative or positive comment goes around and around in a person's head all night.

4. How to have good body language and persuade people

How to have good body language.

A workshop to discuss body language and persuasion. Nonverbal behaviour, or body language, is a language, so think about it as a form of communication. Your everyday body language is often what determines whether people like or trust you. When someone has made up their mind about you, it's all but impossible to change; therefore, body language has to work for you.

Consider the five following common mistakes.

1. A firm handshake. A firm handshake makes an essential first impression. A firm grip displays confidence and establishes you as someone to be taken seriously.

2. Meet someone's eyes. A failure to look someone directly in the eye makes you seem shifty and untrustworthy. But too much eye contact can put off some people. If you want to hold someone's gaze, look at the point just above their nose between their eyes. To the other person, it appears as if you are looking directly into their eyes.

3. Hand gestures. Your hands can be used to enhance words. But don't fuss as this can make you look nervous, distracted, bored or rude.

4. Crossing your arms. This says you are on the defensive, it's a sign of disinterest, being closed off and unapproachable.

5. Nodding too much. You can't be taken seriously if you nod too much. Even when agreeing with what's being said, nodding can be off-putting. It is however, a very good way to show that you are listening, but you need to be subtle

Russell Futcher

How to persuade people.

A primary management activity is the ability to persuade people to do things they either don't want to, are scared of or think they will fail at. The key to persuasion is motivation.

1. Tell them having a go is what's really important.
2. Talk about what they'll lose if they don't do the activity.
3. Draw on their past actions as examples of their ability.
4. Tell them that nearly everyone is doing it or soon will be.
5. Use "we" to include yourself as an involved party in the activity.
6. Ask for a 100 when you only want 10.
7. Talk about the counterargument before they do, that is, the pros and cons of doing the activity.

Practicing and measuring success.

1. Where can the techniques be practiced?
2. How will you know if the techniques are working?
3. How will you know when the techniques have become habits?

5. How to develop charisma and your emotional intelligence

How to develop charisma.

A workshop to discuss how to develop charisma. Charisma is believed to be an innate personality trait that cannot be learned, you either have it, or you don't. However, a manager that possesses gusto and alacrity, is curious and always upbeat in front of staff can be perceived as being charismatic or possessing what I call resonance. Putting forward a positivity attitude also infects peoples thinking.

One of the strange benefits of being a consultant for 40 plus years and having worked in many workplaces, is that I can tell virtually from the moment I walk in the door, just what sort of workplace it is. I can sense something that I call 'resonance', the energy being produced, the vibe, electricity, vibrations in the air. Resonance is the product of a workplace where the Senior Manager exudes an energy that infects the workplace to the extent that the staff also possess gusto and alacrity. Resonance is a form of charisma. It's when you are present, have emotional buy- in created from being positive and without fear of failure, when you display an attitude of getting things done and no problem is insurmountable.

You can tell if you have resonance.

1. Team members and staff feel energised, motivated and good after speaking with you.
2. Your presence creates a sense of resonance in others.
3. When a team member is asked to come and see you, they exhibit gusto and drop everything and walk fast if not run to wherever you are.

How to develop your emotional intelligence. (EI).

(Be sensitive to staff as if they are your children.)

Emotional intelligence is the ability to identify, assess, and control the emotions of yourself and others. It is the ability to be able to identify and express feelings, perceive and evaluate others' emotions; and use emotions to facilitate thinking.

Russell Futcher

Daniel Goleman, the author of 'Emotional Intelligence', researched models from 181 different job roles from 121 companies and discovered that 67 per cent of the competencies deemed essential for effective performance was "emotional" competencies. Emotional intelligence skills are developed through learning from real experiences.

How to practise your EI.

1. Become more self-aware, pay attention to how emotions are affecting your decisions and actions.
2. Pay particular attention to managing strong emotions such as excitement, anger, frustration and distress.
3. Improve your social skills, be curious.
4. Become more empathetic, listen for sues from people.
5. Work on motivation, its usually lack of confidence and, only self-doubt that stops you doing things.
6. Keep practicing the management techniques to improve your confidence.

Practicing and measuring success.

1. Where and when can the techniques be practiced?
2. How will you know if the techniques are working?
3. How will you know when the techniques have become habits?

> "The transformational leader uses charisma, individualized consideration, and intellectual stimulation to inspire employees to make extraordinary efforts". Bass.

6. Managing conflict

A workshop to openly discuss the risks of not managing disputes. The workshop outcome is an agreed method for resolving conflict.

Conflict is unavoidable, it is also useful and needs to be managed constructively and professionally. A clash of ideas is the beginning of innovative thinking, being overly dominant with your ideas; is being selfish and diminishes creative thinking. No team can progress until all team members absolutely believe that they have a voice that is heard. The team, as a whole, needs to settle and decide between competing ideas.

High-performance teams resolve conflicts professionally and constructively. They focus on extracting value from their differences and use this to arrive at better decisions. They actively thrive on conflicts as they know they can convert them into new opportunities by using the points of difference as new possibilities. Managed, mature conflict is essential, it underpins innovation and creativity.

It makes sense, therefore, to see conflict resolution as a form of debate with an agreed decision-making process if a stalemate occurs.

"In surveys of European and American executives, fully 85 per cent of them acknowledged that they had issues or concerns at work that they were afraid to raise. Afraid of the conflict that would provoke, afraid to get embroiled in arguments that they did not know how to manage and felt that they were bound to lose. So how do we develop the skills that we need? Because it does take skill and practice, too. If we aren't going to be afraid of conflict, we have to see it as thinking, and then we have to get really good at it". Margaret Heffernan.

Problems need to be addressed as they arise. Working out problems as a team builds camaraderie. If the problem is personal, care needs to be taken to ensure that a team member does not feel unfairly judged. Problems need to be dealt with openly and transparently. The Senior Manager is the final arbitrator who needs to resolve a problem calmly and without any team member gaining an undue advantage.
Spirited debates around the table should be encouraged, not denied. A good approach is 'it's not what you say but how you say it'.

Russell Futcher

Says Keith Ferrazzi, CEO of Consulting firm Ferrazzi Greenlight. "Teams do not progress when conversations are too polite, people are not challenged, ideas are not questioned. A lack of candour will inevitably diminish decision making, creating a hierarchical culture where people only speak their minds in private". The firm studied 50 large companies and found the highest-performing teams were the most forthright.

"Conflict is inevitable in a team ... in fact, to achieve synergistic solutions, a variety of ideas and approaches are needed. These are the ingredients for conflict". Susan Gerke, IBM, Leadership Development.

Practicing and measuring success.

1. Can the 'decision making' making process in team behaviours be used as a method to resolve conflicts?
2. Is another or a supplementary method needed to resolve conflicts?
3. Will there be a final arbitrator, or will the team always decide?
4. How will you know if the method is working?
5. How will you know when the method has become habitual?
6. How can you train staff on the same method?

> "Anyone can become angry- that is easy. But to be angry with the right person, to the right degree, at the right time, for the right purpose, and in the right way- that is not easy." – Aristotle, The Nicomachean Ethics.

7. The 80/20 principle

80/20 principle.

A workshop to explore the Pareto principle and its many applications. The Pareto principle suggests that 20 % of your activities will account for 80 % of your results; the principle can be applied in many different ways. The principle makes it clear that It's possible to get the same amount of work done in less time than envisaged or customarily allocated. We can take Pareto's 80/20 rule and apply it to almost any situation.

Examples.

1. 80% of output or results comes from 20% of the input or action.
2. 80% of output or results comes from 20% of employees.
3. 20% of time spent on an activity creates 80% of the productivity.
4. 20% of software development efforts account for 80% of the program's functionality.
5. 20% of project planning accounts for 80% of the project results.
6. 20% of project planning time accounts for 80% of the project scope.
7. 20% of project execution accounts for 80% of the project's deliverables.

Finding the 80/20 ratios for your situation is the key to maximizing performance. Find the services that generate the most value (the 20 percent) and reduce the importance of the (the 80 percent) that only provide marginal benefits. Spend time working on the activities that you can improve significantly with your core skillset. Work hardest on elements that work hardest for you.

Practicing and measuring success.

1. What pertinent, work-based examples can you use to support the technique?
2. When can the team use this technique?
3. When can you use this technique?
4. How will you know when the technique has become a habit?
5. How can you best train staff on the use of the technique?

Mandatory, Highly Desirable, Nice to Have.

Another way of speeding up work output is to classify everything as either mandatory, highly desirable or nice to have. Imagine you are doing a project scoping exercise; each item or task being considered for inclusion should be rated as one of these.

Now assuming you have a fixed end or delivery date for the project, you can quickly estimate and schedule just the mandatory tasks first and then the highly desirables second, continuing until you run out of project effort or duration.

Remember, work contracts to fit in the time we give it, or work expands to fill the time available.

Practicing and measuring success.

1. When can the team use these techniques?
2. When can you use these techniques?
3. What activities can these techniques be used on?
4. How will you know when these techniques have become habits?
5. How can you best train staff on the use of these techniques?

8. Having a go is mandatory

A workshop to discuss meeting expectations and removing the fear of failure.

The workshop outcome should be an agreed approach to removing the fear of failure for staff?

We know we learn by making mistakes. It's when mistakes are repeatedly made that there is a problem.

There is a much more significant and more insidious cause for failure, and that's our self-defeat bought on by fear of not meeting expectations, something we can see if we look hard every day in the workplace. You can see it people's eyes when you give them a task to do that, they are not confident about. They have learned that failure, not meeting what's expected, can be punished.

The punishment can be humiliation, no further work allocation of the type just tried, no promotion, not being given a chance to take on something new or significant. Only negative, resounding thoughts about their lack of ability and possibly their job being at risk resounds in their head. Nothing is more demoralizing than seeing those eyes of failure. Poorly trained managers are at fault here, but unfortunately, often, they are only repeating behaviors that they learned in a former low-performance workplace from a former low performance manager.

Succeeding or failing is not the issue; what is the issue is having a go. The following technique when used with people you are getting to know or to whom you are giving a difficult task that they have no experience or knowledge of to undertake, works well. It is the 'hand' technique.

It works like this; explain the task, what you think the outcome may look like and then deliberately place your hand about 10 centimeters above the floor and say "what's important here is having a go. I don't care if you only achieve this much (then raise your hand a bit higher) or you achieve this much, what I care about is your agreeing to have a go at this task please, not what you achieve."
This is very good at removing the anxiety about their ability to do the task and what your expectation of the outcome might be. Finish up by saying "please come

back in a week and please ask if you need any help." Tell them It's your job to help. This technique is remarkably successful, especially as people get to know you and what you expect of them. Just having a go, giving it a try is what it's all about. The remarkable thing is that in over 90% of cases, 90% of the people excel at the task, 90% of the time.

High-performance staff should be able to be given 'any' task whatsoever irrespective of their skillset, knowledge or experience. Using the 'hand' technique is a great way to get people to work on tasks that expand their abilities and understanding of different areas.

Fear of failure is probably one of the main reasons why we prefer to numb ourselves through inaction rather than move forward. Sometimes we are so afraid of letting others down or disappointing them that their opinions dominate us to the point of paralysis. Other times it is a deep-seated feeling of unworthiness that makes us question our abilities.

Practicing and measuring success.

1. How do you feel about using the 'hand' technique?
2. Is it something the team is willing to try out?
3. How will you know if the technique is working?

9. Smart email

Email is largely noise, it's your choice to join in or not. The workshop outcome should be an agreed way of handing emails. When an email comes in, decide within 10 seconds what needs to be done. The Delete, Delegate, Deal with, Decision approach is perfect for quickly getting through large amounts of email, especially if done in a scheduled, fixed block of time. Next decide where to file the email (if not deleting it), when to come back to it (to carry out the task it contains) or wait (for when you're waiting on someone) and move it to a waitlist with a reminder.

If you open the same email more than once, that's wasteful and consumes a lot of time. Otherwise, all other matters should be held over until Weekly Management Team and staff meetings or 1:1 team member sessions. If people are sending lots of emails and copying others, they are spreading their accountability which is an issue. A method of evaluating team member performance is how often and why they are emailing you.

Things to consider.

1. The best strategy is to control 'when' you check email, not allowing it as an interruption, only significant matters should require your immediate attention.

2. Decide on designated times for checking email, turn off all the alerts and then also manage others' expectations about your response time.

3. Try email timeboxing three times a day to clear the Inbox or delegate the Inbox to an assistant with only necessary emails being passed on to you, this is great for getting back time to focus on more important work.

4. "The most valuable form of communication is face-to-face. The next most valuable is by phone or videoconference. The least valuable form of communication is email and texting". Alex Pentland.

5. Use filters (rules). Use keywords to split the emails into folders that get more or less attention or deleted entirely.

6. The problem of preserving business memory contained in emails.

7. Include a note in your signature to let people know you can't always reply, use a number of standard replies saved as signatures.

8. Every day leave the office with an empty inbox.

9. Use email as fast chat: - try restricting messages and replies to the subject line only.

10. Another option is to stop replying to them. This works; answer only the important ones. Once staff understand that you will not automatically respond to every email, they will either come and see you or ring you if it's that important.

Practicing and measuring success.

1. Do you believe you can get control over email?
2. Will an agreed team approach help?
3. How can you encourage or enforce an agreed approach?
4. How can you remind yourself to follow the approach?

> "One CEO on this topic told her staff not to send emails requiring her to make a decision about something - in order to make a decision she would probably need to ask clarifying questions leading to even more messages in her Inbox. She told her staff to ring her or make an appointment to see her instead." The Age Newspaper.

10. Timeboxing

The workshop outcome should be an agreement on when Timeboxing can best be used.

Timeboxing is a most effective time management technique to speed through work. Timeboxing is simply fixing a set period of time to work on a task or group of tasks. Instead of working on a task until it's done, you commit to working on the task for a specific amount of time instead.

"In time management, timeboxing allocates a fixed time period, called a time box, to each planned activity. Several project management approaches use timeboxing. It is also used for individual use to address personal tasks in a smaller time frame. It often involves having deliverables and deadlines, which will improve the productivity of the user". Wiki.

How to do Timeboxing.

Have a watch, clock, phone, computer, anything that has a clock or timer. Find a Task. The first are tasks that you are having a lot of trouble getting the motivation to start. Usually, these are either big things, like writing a report, then.

1. Consider your goals. Take a few minutes to think about what you want to compete.
2. Set a time. How much time you set is going to depend largely on what your goals for the action are.
3. Set a short time. 15 to 30 minutes maybe, that you know won't be too painful or difficult to commit to.
4. Set a longer time frame. An hour or maybe even two hours if you're feeling motivated, don't go too overboard and burn yourself out.
5. Execute. Remember that practice makes perfect.

Example.

1. Timeboxing is an excellent way of doing project planning. The schedule is divided into a number of separate time periods (timeboxes), with each part having its own deliverables, deadline and budget.

2. Without timeboxing, projects usually work to a fixed scope, such that when it is clear that some deliverables cannot be completed, either the deadline slips (to allow more time) or more people are involved (to do more in the same time). Usually both happen, delivery is late, costs go up, and often quality suffers.

3. With timeboxing, the deadline is fixed, but the scope may be reduced. This focuses work on the most important deliverables. For this reason, timeboxing depends on the prioritisation of deliverables, to ensure that it is the project stakeholders who determine the important deliverables rather than software developers.

Practicing and measuring success.

1. Where and when can this technique be best used?
2. How will you know if the technique is working?
3. How will you know if the technique has become a common practice?

> "Work expands to fill the time allotted for its completion." Parkinson's Law.

11. The half pager

A workshop to discuss a potentially contentious, time saving method for writing management submissions.

The workshop outcome would be an addition to the Team Rules to use this method making it mandatory.

This technique restricts all (non-template) management submissions for things such as expenditure approvals, draft project proposals to be limited to a half a page or one whole page as a major exception.

There is no matter or issue that requires more than half a page to explain it. High-performance people understand how time-consuming reading is and aim to reduce the time required. They also understand that being brief makes for a better argument or content.

When you only have a half page to use, it focuses the mind, you only say the salient things which are the same things the reader actually wants to know about, and it keeps you on point. They are fast to read, analyse, decide upon, and you can provide a quick turnaround.

Subordinate and inexperienced staff often feel that the more they write, the stronger their argument will be when, in fact, the opposite is true. Teaching yourself and them to be short and concise helps everyone. It's a fact that the more senior a manager or executive is, the less information they expect to receive. They want to know only the key points of a matter. Make it a Team Rule and advise staff that you won't read anything longer than a half page.

Consider applying a similar rule to emails as well and specify a two-paragraph maximum, or preferably just one or two lines.

Practicing and measuring success.
1. Is this a technique the team will implement as a mandatory rule?
2. Can it be implemented as a general rule rather than a mandatory rule?
3. How will educate staff on what has been decided?

Russell Futcher

12. Problem-solving

A workshop to discuss problem solving techniques. Problem-solving is a creative skill that we often get wrong.
The issue is that as young children we were taught how to solve problems, to systematically break something down, analyse it, look for things, find options, evaluate and select a solution that fixes the problem and hopefully inhibits its repetition. Yet, when you have worked in a developing country as I have where schooling is mostly absent or basic at best, people are not taught how to solve problems as we are, yet they do it every day and more effectively than we do. Over my 40 years, I have dealt with many problems, I have noticed that more often than not, we here in a first world country, highly educated as we are, tend to make problem solving worse simply by the way we have been taught to approach it.

Our brains do it to us. We have taught them that as we encounter the word 'problem', they automatically switch into problem-solving mode, a process that begins by reminding us that problems by and large are negative, something to be avoided or not to be connected with, and that will possibly have personal repercussions. This is the frame of mind with which our well-practised, problem-solving process begins, hardly a good state of mind to start with.

Classic problem solving creates confusion and a lot of background noise generated by too many options, potential solutions, and thoughts about how to protect ourselves from adverse effects. To help matters along, we then produce high levels of anxiety and stress weakening the whole process. In my experience, the answer to nearly every problem is the solution that subconsciously comes to you first. Its correct 90% of the time because there is a very high probability that you already know the answer.

Problems are simply events that need to be dealt with, and thinking about them as events stops the error prone problem-solving process kicking in. Events, which have passed by the time you start thinking about them, are mostly opportunities. I train my team members that there are no problems only new opportunities.

For example, you're a CIO, and you lose an entire health network, its crashed, that's a major event, but once it's happened, it's pointless thinking of it as a problem, the problem has passed. You now have an event, but in restoring it, you need to identify the cause so that you can bring the network back on-line, but also so you can guarantee it won't go down again. That's the opportunity. But if you're in problem-solving mode, you run a high risk of not identifying opportunities because you are focussed only on the underlying cause of the failure and not focussed on preventing that cause from reoccurring. The new opportunity is a solution that most often can be implemented just as fast if not faster than just a problem fix.

I had such a Health network outage once due to router failures, one major router failed and then Murphy's law came into effect and took out another one at the same time. The routers were old but had not failed before and certainly not at the same time. They should have been replaced in the previous year's budget, but the business had rejected funding to replace them even though they had been flagged as high risk. The opportunity was not just replacing these two routers but introducing a new architecture that could then be used to upgrade the performance and reliability of the entire network. Introducing the more modern architecture with different routers was going to take only a little longer than a general fix, but I could guarantee on-going availability, something I couldn't be so sure of if I had only replaced the two failed routers with like for like.

Practicing and measuring success.

1. Where can you improve problem solving?
2. Is a problem manager appointed when a problem occurs in line with SM procedures?
3. Can staff be encouraged to think beyond just a problem fix?

> "Trust your hunches, they're usually based on facts filed away just below the conscious level". Dr Joyce Brothers.

Russell Futcher

13. The art of creativity and innovation

Creative people exhibit 4 common behaviours:

1. They are intensely curious. Curiosity means being able to ask any and every question. Especially the why, where, and what about any subject. This curiosity encourages people them to investigate and look for new, out there, ideas.
2. They connect the dots. Steve Jobs once said creativity is all about connecting the dots. Creative people know how to bounce an idea around and how to bounce ideas off each other until arriving at something new.
3. They ask the big questions. Only by asking big questions can you get big answers. They think well outside what square, they are not constrained by what has been done before.
4. They indulge in daydreaming. They use their imagination, particularly to think about ideas that may seem at first too wild for contemplation. Daydreaming lets lose the power of the mind, to indulge in fantasy and to be innovative.

> "Creativity is just connecting things. When you ask creative people how they did something, they feel a little guilty because they didn't really do it, they just saw something." Steve Jobs. Apple.

It's just about generating enough ideas to solve a problem or create something new. We all have different skills, knowledge and personal attributes. By utilizing all of these various aspects of a team, more ideas can be generated. As more ideas are generated, more creative solutions are generated, leading to better results.

Pick a subject and then brainstorm or better timebox as many solutions and approaches that can be thought of, some will be quite whacky, but these are often the important ones as they prompt ideas in others and can also be connected with other ideas.

> "Always include someone with the biggest imagination so they can give their input, try to bring together imaginative types with inventive types. Someone always had an idea before the things around you that you use every day without thinking about them were created. The ideas that come out of most brainstorming sessions are usually superficial, trivial, and not very original. They are rarely useful. The process, however, seems to make uncreative people feel that they are making innovative contributions and that others are listening to them". -A Harvey Block.

One of the reasons high-performance teams are so successful at creativity and innovation is that they allow and foster different points of view, promoting healthy discussion.

> "Innovation in a business context is simply change that adds value. Innovation comes from great ideas and willingness to embrace change. We're quite deliberate with why we chose that definition. If you're working in an organisation and you don't happen to be in the digital team or new product development team, it can seem that innovation is not your job, but anyone is capable of making a change, so it's an inclusive definition. The value part is important as well - one of the most common definitions I see around innovation is about doing something new or doing something differently. I think that's fine if you're looking to have a bit of fun with innovation but if you're working for a company that actually wants to make a difference or turn a profit or have an impact, then that change has to add value". Dr Amantha Imber. Inventium.

Practicing and measuring success.

6. Where and when does creative thinking occur most often with your team?
7. When should it occur?
8. How can you encourage and develop more creative thinking amongst yourselves and staff?

14. Staff training sessions

A workshop to discuss staff training on high-performance behaviours and techniques.

The workshop outcome should be an agreed approach to staff training, which team bonding events will be used and selection of which workshops to use.

Approach.

1. Review the workshops Scope list. Select those the workshops that are appropriate for staff delivery.
2. Determine delivery approach. E.g. One team member delivers specific workshops to all of the teams, or each team member delivers all workshops to their team.
3. Your own and staff's success or failure depends entirely on adopting the behaviours and techniques as normal daily actions.
4. Staff will best implement the behaviours and techniques after the workshops by seeing their managers implementing them. They will copy your behaviours.
5. What pertinent, work-based examples can you use to support each workshops delivery?
6. How will you enforce the new behaviours and techniques?
7. What repercussions will there be, and what management approach will you use for staff who are not changing?
8. It's important to be consistent in the delivery of the workshops, if you start with one a fortnight, it needs to be continued until the end. There is a risk of the workshops falling away. How can you manage this risk?

Things to consider.

1. How did you feel about the workshop delivery and outcomes?
2. Does the workshop delivery need to be improved?
3. How did you remember everything that you learned?
4. How did you make the new behaviours and techniques habits?

High-Performance Teams

5. Your training consisted of three change forums. 1) Management team meeting. 2) 1:1 Mentoring session and 3) Workshops. How can you adapt your Team meetings to support normalisation of the techniques into daily work activities?
6. Are you holding 1:1 staff mentoring sessions?
7. You could engage an external trainer to deliver the workshops.

Russell Futcher

Team bonding events

The workshops by their nature will facilitate a high degree of team bonding but this is mainly at the professional and intellectual levels. team members need to do some left field team bonding exercises to get them to think outside the box, to learn more about each other as people and to start to move towards a team attitude of 'one for all and all for one'.

At least three team bonding events (if not more) need to be forward planned and scheduled during the first 6 to 9 months to run in parallel with the team building workshops that follow. Included is a recommendation for a high-impact exercise that is very potent in teaching advanced, high-value information communication skills and doing so in incredibly quick time.

Team get togethers.

Holding regular, say monthly team dinners or lunches is incredibly important for the purpose of recognising successes and the team's cohesion. Also celebrate 'Wins', I can't emphasise how important this is both as recognition and motivation.

Outdoors.

These can be as simple as a one to two-day nature trail hike, a water park experience or an adrenaline adventure. Do not do these on week-ends as this interferes with the team members family or personal life activities and commitments.

Personality Tests.

Fun workshops to help each team member better understand each other's strengths and weaknesses. They provide an opportunity for team members to open up about themselves and learn about their respective work styles. They give insight into team member psychological profiles, management styles and work preferences. The easiest and no doubt, the most popular test to undertake is the Myers Briggs Type Indicator questionnaire. It is all about working styles. The personality test is best run by an external provider.

After the Myers Briggs, three other tests are recommended.

High-Performance Teams

1. The Sixteen Personality Factor Questionnaire.
2. The Occupational Personality Questionnaire.
3. The Hogan Personality Inventory.

These indicate the 'working style' favoured by a team member and how they interact with their environment and fellow workers.

5-minute communication exercise.

Team members often know little about each other. This little exercise is very powerful at socialising the team members. In pairs, one person speaks for 5 minutes continuously about anything they like except for work. The other person listens intently and does not interrupt. Then reverse and continue until all team members have spoken to each other.

Advanced Communication exercise.

The gold standard in high-impact exercises, is from Beechwood International. Explain that you are building a high-performance team and let them take it from there. Their solution will be in-house. I have no financial interests in Beechwood; I recommend them as I have been the recipient of their exercises. They are simple and brilliant and the most amazing fun.

"We help leaders realise ambitious goals in an environment of ever-increasing initiative, information and interaction overload, where most people are primarily influenced by where they are, not where they could be. Our approach aims to lighten the burden not add to the problem, take the line of least resistance (we have been likened to a Trojan horse), and recognise that 'we are all customers and suppliers". Beechwood International.

Russell Futcher

Evaluate the team's performance

This is a good time to take stock of what has been achieved to date and to evaluate progress. This evaluation assumes you have completed the workshops and are at least 50% of the way through the change management project. Complete this evaluation with your team members.

Evaluation questions.	Result.
1. Are team members starting to demonstrate gusto and alacrity?	
2. Have they taken up empowerment without it being pushed on to them?	
3. Are they acting in accordance with the team rules?	
4. Are they acting in accordance with the team behaviours?	
5. Does the common goal motivate them?	
6. Are their staff starting to emulate them?	
7. Have team members started to train their staff?	
8. Are the top 20% of business staff starting to stand out?	
9. Have team members developed their own management style?	
10. Is their evidence of mutual trust? (team members are showing signs that they trust each other at the emotional level by sharing fears and weaknesses.)	
11. Is their evidence of mutual accountability? (Once a team decision has been made, each team member feels confident that they are all committed and accountable to each other for the decision.)	
12. Is their evidence of a lack of conflict? (team members should be disagreeing and challenging each other without fear of rebuke.)	
13. Is their evidence of collaboration? (Better, new ideas are emerging.)	

14. Is their evidence that a good decision-making process is in place?	
15. Are the team members accepting an increased workload? (Normal workload plus Change Management Project without additional resources.)	
16. Are team members assisting other team members to complete their tasks?	
17. Are team members practising mutually beneficial and honest communication?	
18. Is the team practising shared leadership? (Where the whole team decides everything together.)	
19. Are team members ignoring their job descriptions? (Thinking and acting outside their job descriptions, when they encounter situations that require action, they act irrespective of their role or position.)	
20. Are team members pulling their sleeves up? (When the going gets tough they recognise that they have to become serious and change their behaviour accordingly.)	
21. Are team members appraising others in public?	
22. Are team members self-motivated? (Possessed of an overwhelming need to be successful and work to achieve it.)	
23. Do team members recognise the need to be process-driven?	
24. Are team members practising the workshop techniques?	
25. Has the team become fully empowered?	

The team may be doing well in some areas and not as well in others, this is the ordinary course of events; what's important is that there is evidence of material change starting to emerge both with team members and with staff.

High-Performance Teams.

Chapter Six. Summary

"I've learned that people will forget what you said, people will forget what you did, but people will never forget how you made them feel." Maya Angelou.

"Perfection is not attainable, but if we chase perfection, we can catch excellence." Vince Lombardi.

"Strive not to be a success, but rather to be of value." Albert Einstein.

I chose these three quotations as they sum up the books content about people, change and outcomes.

Management is all about our interrelationships with people. Within our professional sphere, most of us seek out someone who we see as a people leader, someone who takes an interest in us, that we are happy to follow, be loyal to and who makes us feel good about ourselves. High-performance management is all about people leadership skills, being that leader that others are seeking out.

As the management development process has shown you, it's really not difficult to achieve such a position. It's a process, that with practice builds a management persona, that quickly becomes subconscious and normal.

Fully empower your team members

You may have been micromanaging team members through the high-performance development process. However, with the team common goal, roles/responsibilities matrix, performance goals, team rules and team behaviours in place, and with the workshops well underway or completed, you should consider team members to now be fully empowered. This means that they are now personally and mutually accountable for their actions. It's time to consider informing the team that you are loosening the reins, allowing them how to decide how to do their jobs entirely. Providing autonomy gives team members the freedom to think freely and bring better ideas to the table. Such ideas ideally will be directed at increasing productivity, efficiency and profits.

Fully empowering team members is something that will enhance creativity and their feeling of being genuinely professional; it will also bolster the team as a whole. This is an excellent opportunity to tell M embers about your expectations of supporting their staff, raising customer satisfaction levels, producing higher quality work and meeting agreed timeframes or SLA's. If you are well into the change management project by this time, then you should add that you expect an increased workload to be delivered.

Giving full empowerment means accepting mistakes (but not the same mistake repeated) and less need for mentoring on your part. A good measure of how empowered they feel and how they have embraced their new freedom is the number of emails being they send to you seeking an opinion or approval. If you can, complete the empowerment process by establishing an 'Operating Authority' (a financial expenditure amount) for each team member.

> It's essential now that your messages to the team are consistent with the change management project outcomes being sought. Namely that all work is process-driven, the intranet is the only single source of truth, that the general management approach is to be risk aware and risk-averse, that team rules and behaviours are to be followed, that the common goal directs all activities, and that staff morale is paramount. Keep selling these messages as often as you can to all staff.

Continuous support and motivation

Every time you speak with a team member is an opportunity to provide feedback on their performance and to offer support and motivation. Everyone needs to receive positive feedback so that they understand that they are important, are a contributor, a team player and believe they are receiving an honest assessment of their performance. Everyone knows when they are doing well and when they are doing poorly, you need to recognise and discuss their situation with them.

Russell Futcher

Every time, without fail that I have a discussion with a Team or staff member and especially when I have given them a new task, I always ask "What can I do to help?". I have found this to be enormously influential in showing my support for them and my eagerness that they are successful. Try it, it works. Adding appropriate feedback, supportive and motivational comments adds substantially to feelings of job satisfaction. Lack of job satisfaction is always one of the top three issues in employee surveys.

> One of the most important management functions is to support and motivate team members. A negative or positive comment goes around and around in a person's head all night.

Increase the workload

As the team members begin to settle in to their new ways of working it is time to start exploiting their new collective consciousness. By the time you have completed workshops, it is the time to increase the workload. Provided you are comfortable that team members are sharing information, collaborating and are mutually accountable and openly and honestly communicating then they are ready to handle increased levels of pressure stretching them to higher levels of performance.

Take a notepad and whatever time is necessary to do a business walkaround and speak to as many staff as possible about how things are going. (Make a joke about the fact that you can't remember their names and always ask "what is your number one issue."). The real purpose of the walkaround is to gauge for yourself the level of staff morale and perception as to job satisfaction and how busy they are. Try to frame questions to help you ascertain their use of the new behaviours and techniques. If you come away with a good feeling, then it's not only time, but essential that you increase the workload for everyone.

To reiterate

All your work will be for nothing if you don't increase the workload. Only an increased workload will take what was just another team, over the last hurdle or fence to get to the high-performance team side. Busy people achieve more, and the fuel for a high-performance team is workload.

Without a consistently high workload, a high-performance team will simply not perform as designed or expected.

A high workload brings into daily practice the use of the new management practices, behaviours and techniques. It has the effect of causing all involved to be more reliant on each other, more trusting, more committed and mutually accountable for all their work. It enforces the adherence to process, facilitates true collaboration, it gets more people involved with a task when necessary, each of whom is committed to its success and it forges close work bonds and a prevailing attitude of 'all for one and one for all'.

Key things to remember

1. It does not take much to support and motivate people, just doing this alone yields substantial results.
2. Management style is an individual thing, a persona that we create, that we are comfortable with. We all have different management personas.
3. Your people will copy what you say and how you act.
4. Having the 'right' people in your management team is one of your key success factors. Don't settle for second best, there is no need, there are great people out there.
5. Most people are capable of achieving high-performance status, give everyone a chance to show you what they can do.
6. Recruit people better than yourself, noting that university/college level qualifications are not necessary.
7. Change effects everyone differently, be patient with people, most respond favourably.
8. The workshops are everyone's opportunity to express their needs and feelings.
9. Achieving the workshop outcomes is the name of the game.

10. The management practices, behaviours and techniques are management tools.
11. Equipped with these tools, people excel when empowered.
12. The management tools combined with workload is the secret to success, it takes what was just another team over the fence to become a high-performance team.

End.

High-Performance Teams.

Appendix A.   Team Roles/Responsibilities Matrix

Name. Position.	Name Infrastructure Manager	Name Technical Services Team Leader	Name Networking	Name Desktop Team Leader	Name Capacity Mgt Team Leader
Goals/KPIs. Individual performance goals.	Staff training program. Infrastructure strategic plan. Disaster Recovery testing.	Server availability. Server recovery <1 hour.	Networking architecture review.	SOE standardization.	Capacity Management software installation.
Accountabilities. Personal, key position accountabilities	Systems availability. Infrastructure assets. Disaster Recovery. Managed Services contract.	Level 2 support. Architecture compliance. Server 99.9% availability.	Level 2 support. Architecture compliance. Network 99.9% availability.	Level 2 support. Architecture compliance. Desktop maintenance. 99.9% availability.	Level 2 support. Architecture compliance. Server Performance Management. 99.9% availability.
Responsibilities. Shared responsibilities for applications /systems names.	Application names. Systems names. Other.	Application names. Systems names. Other.	Application names. Systems names. Other.	Application names. Systems names. Other.	Application names. Systems names. Other.
Second in charge.	Name of person	Name of person	Name of person	Name of person	Name of person

Russell Futcher

Name of 2IC.	second in charge.	second in charge.	second in charge.	second in charge.	second in charge.
Roles. Names of secondary roles held by this position.	CAB Chairperson.		Security officer.	Business liaison officer.	
Ownership. Owner and decision maker for these applications/ systems/assets.	Application names. Systems names. Other.	Application names. Systems names. Other.	Application names. Systems names. Other.	Application names. Systems names. Other.	Application names. Systems names. Other.
Expertise. Has knowledge /experience of these applications/systems.	Application names. Systems names. Other.	Application names. Systems names. Other.	Application names. Systems names. Other.	Application names. Systems names. Other.	Application names. Systems names. Other.
Courses completed. Completed courses.	Course names.	Course names.	Course names.	Course names.	Course names.
Courses to do. Names of courses to be completed.	Course type.	Course type.	Course type.	Course type.	Course type.

High-Performance Teams

Appendix B. Staff Survey Questions

Listed below, are some statements that could be used to describe your workplace. Please read each statement carefully and indicate the extent to which you 'agree' or disagree' that the statement applies at the present time by marking the appropriate response.

COMMUNICATION		Strongly Disagree			Strongly Agree	
1	There is an effective flow of information in all directions	1	2	3	4	5
2	I often receive critical information too late	1	2	3	4	5
3	There are forums in this workplace where I can express my views and opinions	1	2	3	4	5
4	Our organization keeps us informed about current developments	1	2	3	4	5
5	There is good communication between departments within this organization	1	2	3	4	5
6	Changes in my work are well communicated to me	1	2	3	4	5
7	There is a common goal that my team is working towards	1	2	3	4	5
FEEDBACK & RECOGNITION						
8	I receive feedback on my performance in a timely and appropriate manner	1	2	3	4	5
9	I believe that I am rewarded fairly for the work I do	1	2	3	4	5
10	Our organization has an effective performance appraisal system in place	1	2	3	4	5
ORGANISATIONAL STRUCTURE						
11	I have access to all required resources necessary to complete projects	1	2	3	4	5

12	I am clear of what my role is within this organization	1	2	3	4	5
13	Management sends a clear message that quality is important in this organization.	1	2	3	4	5
14	There are good linkages between teams, that allows the smooth flow of activities	1	2	3	4	5
15	In my opinion, there is too much duplication of effort within this department	1	2	3	4	5
16	I am satisfied with the hours that I am currently working	1	2	3	4	5
17	I do not think that management will act on this survey	1	2	3	4	5
MANAGEMENT & SUPPORT		Strongly Disagree			Strongly Agree	
18	My manager has a clear vision of where the team is going	1	2	3	4	5
19	People are treated with respect in our team regardless of their level	1	2	3	4	5
20	My manager must tolerate substandard performance, to meet goals, budgets and quotas	1	2	3	4	5
21	I can approach my manager to discuss concerns and grievances	1	2	3	4	5
22	Management does not really know what problems staff are experiencing in their working lives	1	2	3	4	5
23	If I am dissatisfied with my manager's decisions on an issue, I feel free to go to someone higher in authority	1	2	3	4	5
EMPLOYMENT ISSUES						
24	It is difficult for me to gain access to the	1	2	3	4	5

High-Performance Teams

	training that I need or want					
25	When job or work processes change, there is appropriate training available	1	2	3	4	5
26	At times, I am anxious over the security of my job at this organization	1	2	3	4	5
27	I think that this organization offers me long-term career opportunities	1	2	3	4	5
28	There is a clear career path within this organization	1	2	3	4	5
29	This organization allows me to adequately balance my work and family life	1	2	3	4	5
TEAMWORK						
30	I enjoy working in a team environment	1	2	3	4	5
31	There is good cooperation between my team and other teams within the organization	1	2	3	4	5
32	My team needs to focus on fewer activities	1	2	3	4	5
33	We need to meet more often as a team	1	2	3	4	5
34	There is little planning in my team	1	2	3	4	5
35	All team members take equal responsibility	1	2	3	4	5
36	Those who are permanent staff are more committed to team performance than contractual employees.	1	2	3	4	5
MORALE		Strongly Disagree			Strongly Agree	
37	My contribution at work is valued	1	2	3	4	5
38	My dissatisfaction with this job has led me to consider quitting	1	2	3	4	5
39	The morale amongst staff in this organization is low	1	2	3	4	5

| 40 | My co-workers offer support and encouragement to help each other succeed | 1 | 2 | 3 | 4 | 5 |

www.ingramcontent.com/pod-product-compliance
Lightning Source LLC
Chambersburg PA
CBHW050006230526
45465CB00003BB/1282